Reading & Writing
Petra

NATIONAL GEOGRAPHIC
LEARNING

Australia • Brazil • Mexico • Singapore • United Kingdom • United States

National Geographic Learning,
a Cengage Company

Reading & Writing, Petra

**Lauri Blass, Mari Vargo, Keith S. Folse,
April Muchmore-Vokoun, Elena Vestri**

Publisher: Sherrise Roehr

Executive Editor: Laura LeDréan

Managing Editor: Jennifer Monaghan

Digital Implementation Manager,
Irene Boixareu

Senior Media Researcher: Leila Hishmeh

Director of Global Marketing: Ian Martin

Regional Sales and National Account
Manager: Andrew O'Shea

Content Project Manager: Ruth Moore

Senior Designer: Lisa Trager

Manufacturing Planner: Mary Beth
Hennebury

Composition: Lumina Datamatics

For permission to use material from this text or product,
submit all requests online at **cengage.com/permissions**
Further permissions questions can be emailed to
permissionrequest@cengage.com

Student Edition: Reading & Writing, Petra
ISBN-13: 978-0-357-13835-9

National Geographic Learning
20 Channel Center Street
Boston, MA 02210
USA

Locate your local office at **international.cengage.com/region**

Visit National Geographic Learning online at **ELTNGL.com**
Visit our corporate website at **www.cengage.com**

Printed in China
Print Number: 02   Print Year: 2019

PHOTO CREDITS

Scope and Sequence

Unit Title and Theme	Reading Texts and Video	ACADEMIC SKILLS Reading
1 **THE TRAVEL BUSINESS** *page 1* ACADEMIC TRACK: Economics/Business	**Reading 1** The New Face of Tourism **VIDEO** Galápagos Tourism **Reading 2** Geotourism in Action	**Focus** Analyzing Causes and Effects Predicting, Understanding Key Terms, Understanding Main Ideas, Understanding Purpose, Identifying Arguments, Skimming, Understanding Details, Inferring Meaning

Unit Title and Theme	Writing	Grammar for Writing
2 **CAUSE-EFFECT ESSAYS** *page 24*	What Is a Cause-Effect Essay? Example Cause-Effect Essays Developing a Cause-Effect Essay Choosing Words Carefully Developing Ideas for Writing	Connectors for Cause-Effect Essays Connectors That Show Cause Connectors That Show Effect Noun Clauses

Unit Title and Theme	Reading Text and Video	ACADEMIC SKILLS Reading
3 **CHANGING THE PLANET** *page 49* ACADEMIC TRACK: Environmental Studies	**Reading** The Human Age by Elizabeth Kolbert (argumentative essay) **VIDEO** Trees of Life	**Focus** Understanding Cohesion Understanding Main Ideas and Details, Understanding Infographics

Unit Title and Theme	Reading Texts and Video	ACADEMIC SKILLS Reading
4 **MEDICAL INNOVATIONS** *page 73* ACADEMIC TRACK: Health/Medicine	**Reading 1** The Healer of Córdoba **VIDEO** Healthcare Innovator **Reading 2** Medical Frontiers	**Focus** Understanding Passive Sentences Predicting, Summarizing, Identifying Main Ideas, Sequencing, Understanding Details, Inferring Meaning, Understanding Referencing

VOCABULARY EXTENSION 92   BRIEF WRITER'S HANDBOOK 95

Critical Thinking	Writing	Vocabulary Extension
Focus Evaluating Arguments Synthesizing, Evaluating/Justifying	**Skill Focus** Writing a Cause-Effect Essay **Language for Writing** Using *if* … , (*then*) … **Writing Goal** Revise parts of a cause and effect essay	**Word Forms** Adjectives and Nouns ending in -*ive*

Building Better Vocabulary	Original Student Writing	
Word Associations Using Collocations	**Original Student Writing** Write a Cause-Effect Essay **Photo Topic** Write about some effects of extreme weather. **Timed Writing Topic** Why do people keep pets?	

Critical Thinking	Writing	Vocabulary Extension
Focus Analyzing Evidence Evaluating, Synthesizing, Guessing Meaning from Context	**Skill Focus** Reviewing essay writing **Language for Writing** Using cohesive devices **Writing Goal** Revise parts of a cause and effect essay	**Word Forms** Adjectives ending in -*ic* **Word Partners** *dramatic* + noun

Critical Thinking		Vocabulary Extension
Focus Inferring Purpose Reflecting, Applying, Synthesizing		**Word Partners** Antonyms

THE TRAVEL BUSINESS 1

In 2016, more than 5 million people visited Abu Dhabi's Sheikh Zayed Grand Mosque.

ACADEMIC SKILLS

READING	Analyzing causes and effects
WRITING	Writing a cause-effect essay
GRAMMAR	Using *if ..., (then) ...*
CRITICAL THINKING	Evaluating arguments

THINK AND DISCUSS

1 What benefits can tourism bring to a city?
2 What problems can tourism cause?

A Look at the information on these pages and answer the questions.

1. Look at the list of the top most visited cities. Why do you think so many people go to those places?

2. What are some positive effects of mass tourism?

B Match the words in yellow to their definitions.

_____ (v) to keep in good condition

_____ (n) the system by which a government's industry and money are organized

_____ (adj) special; very different

Osaka was the world's 17th most popular destination in 2016. Among the city's most distinctive landmarks is Shitennō-ji—one of the oldest temples in Japan.

Top 10 destination cities by international overnight visitors (2016)

1 Bangkok 21.5 million	**4** Dubai 15.3 million	**5** New York 12.8 million	**6** Singapore 12.1 million
2 London 19.9 million	**7** Kuala Lumpur 12.0 million	**9** Tokyo 11.7 million	**10** Seoul 10.2 million
3 Paris 18.0 million	**8** Istanbul 12.0 million		

TRENDS IN TRAVEL

A recent study of global travel shows some surprising trends. While Paris and London have always been popular with businesspeople and tourists, the world's most visited city is Bangkok, which had over 21 million overnight travelers in 2016. The fastest-growing destination in terms of visitors who stay overnight is Osaka. In terms of how much money visitors spend in the city, Dubai ranks number one—visitors spent over $31 billion there in 2016.

For many of these destinations, mass tourism—large groups of people visiting popular destinations on organized trips—is critical to the success of their **economy**. Tourists spend money at hotels, shops, restaurants, and attractions—providing jobs for thousands of people. Tourism dollars also help cities build and **maintain** roads, parks, and other amenities, which benefit both visitors and locals.

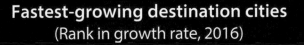

Fastest-growing destination cities
(Rank in growth rate, 2016)

1	2	3
Osaka	Chengdu	Abu Dhabi

Reading 1

PREPARING TO READ

BUILDING
VOCABULARY **A** The words and phrases in **blue** below are used in Reading 1. Read the paragraph. Then match the correct form of each word or phrase to its definition.

Mass tourism isn't the only way to travel. One **alternative** is to experience another country by studying there. Many universities form **partnerships** with schools in other parts of the world to allow their students to learn about other cultures. Overseas students may also choose to stay in their host country during vacations, particularly if they are able to **earn a living** through part-time jobs, such as working in a café or restaurant.

1. _____ (v) to get money to pay for things that you need

2. _____ (n) a way of working with another person, group, or organization

3. _____ (n) something you can choose instead of another thing

BUILDING
VOCABULARY **B** Read the sentences. Choose the best definitions for the words in **blue**.

1. Many cities **preserve** their historic buildings, so tourists can see how the city used to look.
   a. to make additional copies of   b. to protect from harm

2. It may be **necessary** to get a visa before you are allowed to enter a country.
   a. essential; required   b. useful; recommended

3. Economic development must be **sustainable** in order to benefit future generations.
   a. able to continue in the long term   b. able to affect many places

4. Mass tourism can have **harmful** effects on cities, such as increasing pollution levels.
   a. unusual; surprising   b. damaging; dangerous

USING
VOCABULARY **C** Discuss these questions with a partner.

1. What are some **distinctive** travel destinations in your country or region?

2. Which historic places or buildings in your area have been **preserved**?

BRAINSTORMING **D** What are the positive and negative effects of large numbers of tourists visiting a natural area, such as a beach or a forest? Discuss with a partner.

PREDICTING **E** Read the first paragraph of the reading passage. The prefix *geo-* refers to the Earth. How do you think "geotourism" is different from mass tourism? Check your ideas as you read.

THE NEW FACE OF TOURISM

Track 1

A The twenty-first century has seen significant growth in mass tourism. This growth brings an increased risk of endangering the sites that make a place unique and worth visiting. However, a new kind of tourism approach—geotourism—may offer a solution.

B Jonathan Tourtellot is founding director of the Destination Stewardship Center. Its mission is to protect and maintain the world's distinctive places through wisely managed tourism. Tourtellot is an advocate of the *geotourism* approach, a term he came up with to describe the core strategy for achieving this goal. He believes that as mass tourism continues to grow and move into places that saw few visitors in the past, geotourism will be a good long-term plan. "The challenge of managing tourism in a way that protects places instead of overrunning[1] them," says Tourtellot, "is simply going to become larger."

C Geotourism is an alternative to mass tourism, which can have harmful effects on local people and on the environment. Many of the systems that support mass tourism—large hotels, chain restaurants,[2] tour companies—are often owned and run by companies based outside the tourist areas. Chain restaurants may not always serve local food. Large tour companies do not always hire local experts and guides, even though these people might have the most insight into the area's history and culture. Much of the money made from this type of tourism does not, therefore, benefit the local economy. In addition, with mass tourism, visitors do not usually have much contact with the local people. This limits their understanding of the nature and culture of the places they visit.

D In contrast, geotourism is like a partnership between travelers and locals. For example, geotravelers stay in hotels owned by local residents who care about protecting the area and the environment. Geotravelers eat in restaurants that serve regional dishes. They buy from local merchants and craftspeople and hire local travel guides. They also try to see traditional music, dance, and theater. As a result, these travelers gain a broader understanding of the area's history and culture. Moreover, the money they spend stays in the local community. This helps local people earn a living; it is also necessary in order to protect the area for future travelers. In this way, geotourism benefits both sides of the partnership—the travelers and the locals.

[1]If a place is **overrun**, it is fully occupied.
[2]**Chain restaurants** are owned by the same company and have standardized products and services.

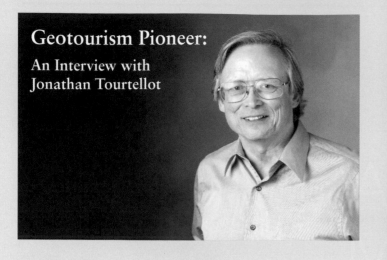

Geotourism Pioneer:
An Interview with Jonathan Tourtellot

Q: How would you differentiate among ecotourism, sustainable tourism, and geotourism?

E **Tourtellot:** Ecotourism focuses specifically on natural areas. I'm convinced that there are elephants roaming Africa and trees growing in Costa Rica that would not be there without ecotourism. Sustainable tourism ... seems to say, "Keep everything the way it is." We needed a term that would bring the ecotourism principle out of its niche[3] and cover everything that makes travel interesting. Geotourism is defined as tourism that sustains or enhances the geographical character of a place—the environment, heritage, aesthetics,[4] culture, and well-being of local people.

Q: What happens when tourism is badly managed?

F **Tourtellot:** It can destroy a place. Coasts, for example, are extremely vulnerable. Coasts are important for biodiversity because much of marine life has its nurseries[5] in coastline areas. So development there is a highly sensitive issue. Same thing goes for attractive mountainsides like the Rockies of the West. That's why when development occurs on a large scale, it's important that it be ... well planned.

Q: What happens to a destination after years of heavy traffic?

G **Tourtellot:** Here's an example—at the Petrified Forest [in northeast Arizona], it's very easy to bend down, pick up a little bit of petrified wood, and pocket it. People think it's only one pebble[6] in such a vast area, so it makes no difference if they take it. But since millions of visitors over the years have thought the same thing, all of the pebbles have disappeared—meaning there's been an enormous loss of what makes the Petrified Forest so special. So, when you're talking about an entire location like a town, a stretch of coastline, a wild area, or a national park, it's important to listen to park rangers when they tell you where to go and not go, what to do and not do.

---

[3] A **niche** is a special area of demand for a product or a service.
[4] **Aesthetics** relates to the appreciation and study of beauty.
[5] Marine-life **nurseries** are places where young sea creatures can begin growing into adults.

[6] A **pebble** is a small, round stone.

According to a survey by the Destination Stewardship Center, the Norwegian Fjords are one of the world's best examples of geotourism.

Q: What happens when tourism is managed well?

Tourtellot: It can save a place. When people come [to] see something special and unique to an area—its nature, historic structures, great cultural events, beautiful landscapes, even special cuisine—they are enjoying and learning more about a destination's geographical character … Travelers spend their money in a way that helps maintain the geographical diversity and distinctiveness of the place they're visiting. It can be as simple as spending your money at a little restaurant that serves a regional dish with ingredients from local farmers, rather than at an international franchise[7] that serves the same food you can get back home.

Q: How else can tourism help benefit a destination?

Tourtellot: Great tourism can build something that wasn't there before. My favorite example is the Monterey Bay Aquarium in California. It was built in a restored cannery[8] building on historic Cannery Row—which is a good example of **preserving** a historical building rather than destroying it. The aquarium, which has about 1.8 million visitors each year, brought people's attention to the incredible variety of sea life right off the coast of California. And it played a major role in the development of the Monterey Bay National Marine Sanctuary. Once people saw what was there, they wanted to protect it.

[7] A **franchise** is allowed to sell another company's products.

[8] A **cannery** is a factory where food is canned.

UNDERSTANDING THE READING

A Check (✓) the three best statements to complete the definition of *geotourism*.

According to Jonathan Tourtellot, geotourism _____ .

☐ 1. focuses on bringing people to natural areas

☐ 2. has positive effects on local economies

☐ 3. helps preserve the environment

☐ 4. benefits international tour companies

☐ 5. is good for both travelers and locals

B Check (✓) four statements that summarize Tourtellot's main ideas.

☐ 1. Geotourism is similar to ecotourism, but is mainly concerned with controlling pollution caused by tourists.

☐ 2. Tourism that is not well planned can cause significant environmental damage, particularly along coastlines.

☐ 3. When a place has a lot of visitors over a long period of time, the visitors can destroy some of the characteristics that made the site special.

☐ 4. When tourism is well planned, people learn about the geography of an area and help support it at the same time.

☐ 5. Tourism can help preserve places that might otherwise be lost.

☐ 6. The basic idea of geotourism is "keep everything the way it is."

C Match each place mentioned in the reading passage to the main reason (a–d) Tourtellot mentions it.

_____ 1. Costa Rica

_____ 2. The Rockies

_____ 3. The Petrified Forest

_____ 4. Monterey Bay Aquarium

a. an unusual landscape that has been significantly damaged by tourism

b. a region where careful development planning is important

c. an example of how geotourism can help preserve a historical site

d. a place where ecotourism has had a positive environmental impact

---

CRITICAL THINKING Writers often make arguments by contrasting the advantages of an idea with the disadvantages. You can **evaluate** their argument by asking:

• Is there enough evidence to support each argument?

• Does the writer present both sides of the argument?

• Is the presented evidence fair and up to date?

• Does the evidence relate logically to the argument?

D Complete the notes comparing geotourism and mass tourism with suitable words.

Advantages of Geotourism	Disadvantages of Mass Tourism
• allows tourism growth to be managed in the long term	• does not promote local food or culture
• people support the _____ by using local hotels or restaurants	• people spend money that doesn't go to _____
• visitors gain a deeper understanding of the area's _____	• people gain a limited _____ of the places they visit
• careful development can help preserve _____ and educate people about the area	• unmanaged tourist numbers can cause natural areas to _____ their original beauty

E Work with a partner. Answer the questions below.

1. What might be some disadvantages of geotourism?

   _____

   _____

2. Consider the pros and cons of geotourism and mass tourism (refer to your answers in 1, exercise D, and exercise A-2 in Explore the Theme). Are you convinced by the writer's argument that geotourism is better than mass tourism? Why or why not?

   _____

   _____

The Petrified Forest receives around 800,000 visitors every year.

DEVELOPING READING SKILLS

> **READING SKILL** Analyzing Causes and Effects
>
> Recognizing causes and effects can help you understand a writer's main arguments. The following words and phrases are used to signal cause-effect relationships.
>
> **For introducing causes:**
>
> *if, because of, when, as, one effect of*
>
> **For introducing effects:**
>
> *as a result, one result (of…) is, so, therefore, consequently, (this) leads/led to*
>
>   CAUSE   EFFECT
>
> *Tourism brings money into a community.* **As a result**, *governments can make improvements that benefit local residents.*
>
>   CAUSE   EFFECT
>
> **Because of** *the money brought into a community by tourism, governments can make improvements that benefit local residents.*
>
> Sometimes, writers do not use signal words to show cause-effect relationships; in these cases, you need to infer the meaning from the context.

IDENTIFYING CAUSES AND EFFECTS

A Read the sentences. Underline words that signal causes and circle those that signal effects.

1. As ecotourism can bring many benefits, many local and national governments are looking at ways to preserve their distinctive natural areas.

2. In Costa Rica, for example, an interest in developing ecotourism led to the creation of several national parks and reserves where wildlife is protected.

3. The creation of national parks and reserves requires large numbers of skilled workers. Consequently, many people who are out of work may become employed.

4. The government of Costa Rica created a successful international ecotourism marketing campaign. As a result, tourism to the country increased dramatically.

ANALYZING CAUSES AND EFFECTS

B Complete the chart with the causes and effects of geotourism / mass tourism. Use information from paragraphs C and D in the passage.

Cause	Effect
1.	1. The money made does not help the local economy.
2.	2. People don't know much about the nature and culture of the places they visit.
3. Travelers eat and shop at local businesses.	3.
4. The money spent by travelers goes to the local community.	4.

ANALYZING CAUSES AND EFFECTS

C Which of the cause-effect sentence(s) in paragraphs C and D contained a signal word or phrase? Which required inferring from the context? Discuss with a partner.

Giant land tortoises on
Santa Cruz island, Galápagos

Video

GALÁPAGOS TOURISM

BEFORE VIEWING

A What effect might tourists and tourism activities have on animal species that live on remote islands? Discuss with a partner.

PREDICTING

B Read the information about the Galápagos Islands. Then answer the questions.

LEARNING ABOUT
THE TOPIC

The Galápagos Islands are located 620 miles (1,000 km) off the coast of Ecuador. Thousands of different species live on the islands, many of which cannot be found anywhere else on Earth. The naturalist Charles Darwin studied the animals of the Galápagos—particularly the finches (a bird species) and tortoises. From his study of finches, Darwin saw how animals change to adapt to their environments. This research inspired his development of the theory of evolution, which he described in detail in his 1859 book *On the Origin of Species*. Today, tourists from around the world are able to interact closely with the islands' animals.

1. What is special about the animals on the Galápagos Islands?

   _____

2. How did the Galápagos Islands contribute to our scientific knowledge?

   _____

C The words and phrases in **bold** below are used in the video. Read the sentences. Then match the correct form of each word or phrase to its definition.

> **Contaminants**, such as gasoline and other fuels, can contribute to water pollution.
>
> Tourism can bring **revenue** to a place, but it can also bring problems.
>
> Jonathan Tourtellot believes that by managing tourism, we can avoid **ruining** destinations for future travelers.
>
> A global cyberattack by a computer virus, WannaCry, was a **wake-up call** for many countries to strengthen their cyber security measures.

1. _____ (n) money that a company or an organization receives
2. _____ (n) a substance that makes something unsuitable for use
3. _____ (v) to destroy or severely damage something
4. _____ (n) an event that is serious enough to make people aware of a big problem

WHILE VIEWING

UNDERSTANDING
MAIN IDEAS

A ▶ Watch the video. Check (✓) the main ideas of the video.

☐ 1. Human presence on the islands has increased significantly in the last few decades.
☐ 2. Tourist revenue has been used for some major construction projects on the islands.
☐ 3. Tourism is negatively affecting the natural environment of the islands.
☐ 4. The local people have started adopting more environmentally friendly practices.

UNDERSTANDING
DETAILS

B ▶ Watch the video again. Check (✓) the actions that are being taken to make the islands greener.

☐ 1. Older oil tanks have been replaced with more modern ones.
☐ 2. The number of tourists on the islands has been restricted.
☐ 3. Gas stations have barriers to prevent oil leaks.
☐ 4. Cars will be replaced with vehicles that are more environmentally friendly.
☐ 5. The locals are reducing their waste and recycling more.

AFTER VIEWING

REACTING TO
THE VIDEO

A Read the statements below. Which do you agree with more? Why? Discuss with a partner.

1. Banning tourists from the islands is the most effective way to protect the natural environment.

2. Tourism on the islands should be allowed, as long as more efforts are made to manage its growth.

CRITICAL THINKING:
SYNTHESIZING

B Work with a partner. Can you think of other ways that the environment on the Galápagos Islands could be protected? Use ideas from Reading 1 or your own ideas.

Reading 2

PREPARING TO READ

BUILDING VOCABULARY

A The words in **blue** below are used in Reading 2. Read the paragraphs. Then match the correct form of each word to its definition.

A key **objective** of geotourism is to make sure places are environmentally friendly. Some hotels, for example, not only provide **comfort** to their visitors; they also have sustainable practices such as using **renewable** energy sources like solar power for electricity. Hotel companies are also encouraged to assess the **ecological** impact of any new projects before they start building.

Another **vital** part of geotourism is to raise people's **awareness** of the history and culture of the places they visit. For example, tours may include visits to **landmarks** that have **spiritual** meaning to the local people, such as Chichén Itzá in Mexico, where ceremonies for the gods were often performed. These visits are often more **enriching** when tourists have the chance to interact with local people employed as **official** guides.

1. _____ (n) a goal

2. _____ (n) a state of ease or well-being

3. _____ (n) knowledge that something exists

4. _____ (adj) able to be replaced naturally

5. _____ (adj) necessary or extremely important

6. _____ (adj) providing more appreciation or enjoyment

7. _____ (adj) relating to a government or an organization

8. _____ (n) a building or structure with historical or cultural significance

9. _____ (adj) relating to a higher purpose rather than just material needs

10. _____ (adj) relating to the relationship between living things and their surroundings

USING VOCABULARY

B Think back to the last time you traveled to a new place. What was your main **objective**: to relax, to learn something, to meet people, or something else? Discuss with a partner.

SKIMMING

C Skim the reading passage and answer the questions. Then check your ideas as you read.

1. What types of natural places does the reading passage describe?

_____

2. What do these places have in common? List one or two things.

_____

GEOTOURISM IN ACTION

Visitors at Sacha Lodge, Ecuador, explore a jungle walkway.

🎧 Track 2

A As public awareness grows of the negative effects of mass tourism, more travel companies are providing options that enhance—rather than harm—local cultures and environments. The following examples from around the world show how innovative local programs can promote sustainable tourism that benefits tourists, locals, and the environment.

ECOLODGES IN ECUADOR

B Located in the Amazon basin, Ecuador is one of South America's most popular places for tourists. Ecolodges now provide a sustainable travel option for these tourists. First developed in the 1990s, an ecolodge is a type of hotel that helps local economies and protects the environment. Many of the lodges are built with renewable materials that are found locally. The lodges allow people in the community to sell locally made products to guests; some are also owned and operated by local people.

C Ecolodges not only help local economies and the environment, they also enable visitors to gain a deeper understanding of the region. There are ecolodges throughout the country, so visitors can choose to stay in the rain forest, in the mountains, or at an island beach. Visitors at Sani Lodge in the rain forest, for example, are surrounded by over 500 species of tropical birds and a thousand species of butterflies. In the Andes, guests can go hiking and explore volcanic glaciers. On the Galápagos, visitors can watch giant tortoises lay their eggs.

D These lodges let visitors interact with local people and learn about local culture, too. For example, at some ecolodges, guests learn how to make dishes using local ingredients. At Sani Lodge, local families invite guests into their homes. In 2015, the owners of Sani Lodge won the World Legacy Travel Award for their efforts to promote sustainable tourism. This kind of tourism, says company director Jascivan Carvalho, leads to "a deeper, more enriching experience for travelers, and for locals, whose livelihoods improve."

ADVENTURE TREKKING IN NEPAL

Nepal has been an important trekking destination for over a hundred years. Until recently, however, most tour guides and porters were male. In 1993, three sisters—Lucky, Dicky, and Nicky Chhetri—had an idea. They were running a restaurant and lodge in Pokhara, a popular base for trekkers. When some female guests complained of poor treatment by male porters, the sisters decided to act. They would start their own trekking business—one run by women, for women. They launched their partnership—3 Sisters Adventure Trekking—with two main goals: to give local women

opportunities to work in the tourism industry, and to give female trekkers the choice of female guides for greater comfort and security.

The sisters also created a nonprofit organization—Empowering Women of Nepal (EWN). The organization trains and hires local women as guides. The training program includes classes in English, health, and awareness of ecological issues. At the end of the program, the trainees get on-the-job experience as guides, earning the same wages as male guides. Some graduates of the program use their earnings to continue their education, while others start their own businesses.

These improvements to the women's social and financial situations are good for both their families and the rest of the community. The interaction between local guides and tourists from all over the world creates a vital cultural exchange, too. "I learned to become an ambassador for my country," says one of the graduates of the program.

A local guide from 3 Sisters Adventure Trekking with a trekker on Suriya Peak in Nepal

SURIYA PEAK
5145M
GOSAINKUND
NEPAL

Visitors to Uluru learn about the significance of the monument from a local guide.

CULTURAL TOURS IN AUSTRALIA

Uluru is a giant rock formation that stands in the desert of central Australia. Also known as Ayer's Rock, the famous landmark is an Australian icon and a hot spot for tourists. But for the local Anangu—meaning "we people"—Uluru is the heart of a region where they have lived for more than 20,000 years. Until recently, many visitors came to Uluru with the objective of climbing it. However, the Australian government and several tour companies are asking visitors not to do this. In fact, the government of Australia has now introduced an official policy to stop visitors from climbing the monument.

The concerns over climbing Uluru are partly because it is dangerous—the rock stands nearly 350 meters high (over 1,140 feet) and has steep sides. However, it is also a sacred site for the Anangu people, the traditional owners of the rock. For the Anangu, climbing Uluru is a spiritual experience. The government's and tour companies' efforts have had a positive effect. While 74 percent of visitors climbed Uluru in 1990, that number dropped to less than 30 percent by 2015.

Adventure Tours and SEIT Outback Australia are just two of the companies that work to educate visitors about the culture of Uluru. Some of these tour companies hire indigenous guides who can share the perspectives of the local people. Instead of taking tourists to the top of the rock, tour guides lead tourists around Uluru on the paths that Anangu ancestors walked. The guides tell traditional stories about how the world was born and how people are connected to the land. Through these travel experiences, visitors can leave Uluru culturally richer than when they arrived.

UNDERSTANDING THE READING

A Look at the main ideas (1–6) from the reading passage. Match each section of the passage (a–c) with two main ideas.

UNDERSTANDING MAIN IDEAS

a. Ecolodges in Ecuador
b. Adventure Trekking in Nepal
c. Cultural Tours in Australia

_____ 1. The main focus is on providing employment for local women and services for female travelers.

_____ 2. Visitors stay in a type of hotel accommodation that benefits the environment and the financial well-being of local communities.

_____ 3. An education program helps local people learn skills that they can use in their communities.

_____ 4. Visitors have the opportunity to experience a wide variety of natural environments.

_____ 5. Greater awareness of local concerns has reduced the negative impact of tourism on the site.

_____ 6. Tour guides emphasize how the site is culturally and historically significant for the local people.

B Match each paragraph or section from the passage to the best description (1–7).

UNDERSTANDING DETAILS

| B | C | D | E | F–G | H–I | J |

_____ 1. welcoming visitors into local homes

_____ 2. the evolution of a new type of green travel lodge

_____ 3. a wide variety of environmental experiences on offer

_____ 4. a training program that offers local women a better future

_____ 5. understanding a place from a traditional cultural perspective

_____ 6. the origins of a more gender-balanced approach to trekking

_____ 7. reasons why climbing a sacred landmark is now discouraged

Uluru is one of Australia's most well-known landmarks.

C Find and underline the following words and phrases in **bold** in the reading passage. Use context to identify their meanings. Then write the part of speech and your own definition of each word or phrase.

1. **livelihood** (paragraph D) Part of speech: _____

   Meaning: _____

   _____

2. **ambassador** (paragraph G) Part of speech: _____

   Meaning: _____

   _____

3. **hot spot** (paragraph H) Part of speech: _____

   Meaning: _____

   _____

4. **indigenous** (paragraph J) Part of speech: _____

   Meaning: _____

   _____

D Underline the word(s) that signal a cause-effect relationship in the excerpt below. What effect does ecotourism have on travelers and locals? Discuss with a partner.

Director of the company, Jascivan Carvalho, says that this kind of travel experience can lead to

"a deeper, more enriching experience for travelers, and for locals, whose livelihoods improve."

E Read Jonathan Tourtellot's definition of geotourism from Reading 1. What are some examples from the reading that relate to his definition? Note them in the chart.

"Geotourism is defined as tourism that sustains or enhances the geographical character of a place—the environment, heritage, aesthetics, culture, and well-being of local people."

Ecolodges in Ecuador	Adventure Trekking in Nepal	Cultural Tours in Australia

F Which of the three destinations do you think is the best example of geotourism? Why? Note your ideas and discuss your reasons in a small group.

Place: _____

Reason(s): _____

_____

Writing

EXPLORING WRITTEN ENGLISH

A Read the sentences and underline the part that describes a cause. Circle the part that describes an effect.

NOTICING

1. If tourists stay at large international hotels, they often interact less with locals.

2. Tourists don't necessarily help the local economy if they only eat at chain restaurants.

LANGUAGE FOR WRITING Using *if ..., (then) ...*

One way to express a cause-effect relationship that is generally true is to use sentences with *if*. In these sentences, the *if*-clause introduces a condition or cause that leads to the effect or result expressed in the other clause.

CAUSE   EFFECT
If tourism is managed well, both tourists and local people benefit.

You can reverse the order of the clauses.

EFFECT   CAUSE
Both tourists and local people benefit if tourism is managed well.

You can also use a modal (*can, should, might, must*) in the effect clause.

CAUSE   EFFECT
*If tourism is badly managed, it **can** destroy a place.*

Note: Use a comma when the *if*-clause comes first. Use the present tense in the *if*-clause and the present tense or a modal in the effect clause.

B Underline the sentence in each pair (1–4) that is a cause. Then combine the sentences using *if*-clauses.

1. You buy locally made products. You support the local economy.

   _____

2. Forests and beaches might be ruined. Too many people visit them.

   _____

3. Female trekkers feel more comfortable and safe. The porters are female.

   _____

4. Tourists can learn about local customs. They stay at an ecolodge.

   _____

C Use your own ideas to complete each sentence with a cause or an effect.

1. If _____ , it may harm the environment.

2. If tourists use local guides, _____ .

3. Visitors can have an enriching travel experience if _____ .

4. _____ if you meet locals when you travel.

WRITING SKILL Writing a Cause-Effect Essay

One type of cause-effect essay explains how a situation (a cause) produces another situation (an effect). For example, an essay could explain the effects of population growth on an area. The thesis statement in this type of essay states that the focus is on the effects of a particular cause.

In a cause-effect essay that focuses on effects, each body paragraph includes a topic sentence that states the effect. One body paragraph could focus on the most important effect; the next paragraph could focus on a less important effect. Another way to organize body paragraphs is to focus first on the effects on one group (e.g., humans), and then focus on a different group (e.g., animals) in another paragraph.

A well-developed body paragraph includes at least two supporting ideas that include reasons, facts, and examples to help a reader understand your topic sentence. One strategy for adding effective details is to think about questions (*who, why, when, where, what*) that a reader might have about your topic sentence. If your supporting ideas do not adequately answer these questions, then you should add more details.

ANALYZING A
CAUSE-EFFECT
OUTLINE

D The paragraph outline below is for an essay about how vacation rentals (houses that are rented to tourists) affect cities. Use the notes (1–4) to complete the outline.

1. neighborhood businesses lose money

2. may have to lay off employees or shorten their hours

3. they can harm neighborhoods

4. more vulnerable to burglars

Topic Sentence: *One negative effect of vacation rentals is that* _____ .

Supporting Idea 1: *changes the character of a neighborhood*

Details:

• *neighborhoods become empty on weekdays / during off-peak*

• _____

Supporting Idea 2: _____

Details:

• *local businesses don't have enough customers in off-season*

• _____

E The draft paragraph below is about the effects of the redevelopment of a national park. A reader has noted some questions asking for more information. Add the details (a–d) that the writer could use to improve the paragraph.

IMPROVING A CAUSE-EFFECT PARAGRAPH

One positive effect of the redevelopment of Ghana's Kakum National Park was that it greatly improved the local economy. _____ In the 1990s, Conservation International formed partnerships to make the park more attractive to tourists. _____ These improvements had positive financial effects on the community. _____ When the project was finished, there were many more visitors to the park. _____ This increase in tourism continues to bring money into the local economy.

Why did the park need to be redeveloped?

How was the park made attractive to tourists?

How did the community benefit?

How many more visitors were there?

a. fewer than 1,000 visitors in 1991; over 180,000 a year today
b. local people did the work; the project used local materials
c. had suffered for many years from deforestation and lack of investment
d. built visitors' center, wildlife exhibitions, restaurants, shops, camping facilities, a canopy walk—a special walkway (takes visitors through treetops of rain forest)

F Rewrite the paragraph, inserting the information from the notes in the highlighted spaces.

WRITING A CAUSE-EFFECT PARAGRAPH

REVISING PRACTICE

The draft below is a cause-effect essay about the effects of vacation rentals on cities. Follow the steps to create a better second draft.

1. Add the sentences (a–c) in the most suitable spaces.
   a. In some cities, the vacation rental business has reduced the number of available apartments by 20 to 30 percent.
   b. Vacation rentals also have negative effects on housing in a community.
   c. As a result, they may have to lay off some of their employees or limit their hours.

2. Now fix the following problems (d–f) in the essay.
   d. Correct a mistake with an *if ... , (then) ...* sentence in paragraph B.
   e. Cross out one sentence in paragraph C that does not relate to the essay topic.
   f. Correct a mistake with an *if ... , (then) ...* sentence in paragraph C.

A

In the sharing economy, anyone can be an entrepreneur. People can make money with ridesharing, by renting out their cars, or even by renting out their homes. While allowing people to stay in your home for a few days a month might be a nice way to make some extra money, vacation rentals have negative effects on communities.

B

One negative effect of vacation rentals is that they can harm neighborhoods. For example, they can change the character of neighborhoods, particularly those in popular destinations. Low numbers of tourists on weekdays or in the off-peak season can mean nearly empty neighborhoods, making the areas easy targets for burglars. Vacation rentals can also cause neighborhood businesses to lose money. If vacation rentals are empty for days at a time, so small grocers and other neighborhood businesses don't have a lot of customers. _____

C

_____ First of all, short-term vacation rentals can cause housing shortages, as landlords rent apartments out to tourists instead of making them available to permanent residents. _____ In addition, vacation rentals drive up housing prices in a community. If there are fewer apartments available rents tend to go up, forcing people with average incomes to move outside of the city. Rental companies don't always know everything about the home or apartment owners' backgrounds.

D

Short-term vacation rentals have harmful effects on communities. They can negatively impact the character and economy of a neighborhood, and lead to housing shortages and higher rents. When tourism takes over a neighborhood and drives local residents away, is it even the same place anymore?

EDITING PRACTICE

Read the information below.

In sentences with *if*-clauses that describe general truths, remember:

- that the *if*-clause introduces the condition or cause.
- to use a comma after the *if*-clause when it comes first in a sentence.
- to use the present tense in the *if*-clause, and the present tense or a modal in the effect clause.

Correct one mistake with *if*-clauses in each of the sentences (1–5).

1. If prices are too high people might stop traveling.

2. If travel journalists will write about the importance of protecting destinations, they might educate tourists.

3. If tourists only eat at chain restaurants, they didn't learn anything about local food.

4. Tourists show disrespect to the local culture, if they climb Uluru.

5. Local communities can benefit if tourism will promote local businesses.

UNIT REVIEW

Answer the following questions.

1. What are two things you learned about geotourism?

   _____

   _____

   _____

2. What are some signal words or phrases that introduce causes or effects?

   _____

   _____

   _____

3. Do you remember the meanings of these words? Check (✓) the ones you know. Look back at the unit and review the ones you don't know.

   Reading 1:

   ☐ alternative **AWL**   ☐ distinctive **AWL**   ☐ earn a living

   ☐ economy **AWL**   ☐ harmful   ☐ maintain **AWL**

   ☐ necessary   ☐ partnership **AWL**   ☐ preserve

   ☐ sustainable **AWL**

   Reading 2:

   ☐ awareness **AWL**   ☐ comfort   ☐ ecological

   ☐ enriching   ☐ landmark   ☐ objective **AWL**

   ☐ official   ☐ renewable   ☐ spiritual

   ☐ vital

Cause-Effect Essays

Severe storms caused the Gave de Pau river to overflow and destroy roads in Villelongue, France.

OBJECTIVES To learn how to write a cause-effect essay
To use connectors in cause-effect writing
To understand noun clauses

*Can you write about some
effects of extreme weather?*

What Is a Cause-Effect Essay?

A **cause-effect essay** shows the reader the relationship between something that happens and its consequences, or between actions and results. For example, if too much commercial fishing is allowed in the North Atlantic Ocean (action), the fish population in some areas may diminish or disappear (result). Cause-effect essays can be informative, analytical, and insightful. In addition to being able to write a cause-effect essay, you need to know about this type of writing because you may want to include a single paragraph discussing a cause, an effect, or both in a longer essay you are writing, such as a persuasive or argumentative piece.

In this unit, you will study two kinds of cause-effect essays. Very simply, in one method, the writer focuses on the <u>causes</u> of something. Just think of how many people, when they are given a piece of information, like to analyze the topic and ask the question *Why?* or *How?* This is called the **focus-on-causes** method. In the second method, the writer emphasizes the <u>effects</u> or results of a cause. People who like to think hypothetically—answering the question *What if?*—focus on the outcome of a particular event or action. These writers often write **focus-on-effects** essays.

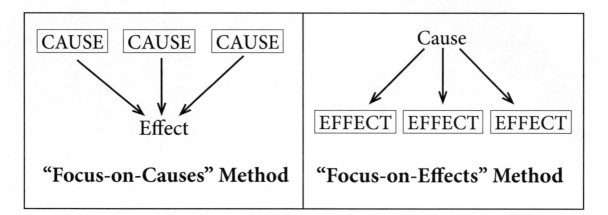

Imagine that your instructor gives you the following writing topic: quitting a job. You have the choice of using the focus-on-causes method or the focus-on-effects method.

Focus-on-causes method: You can choose to write an essay on why people quit their jobs and brainstorm possible reasons they may have for doing so, such as distance from the home or lack of benefits. Each paragraph would contain a different cause.

Focus-on-effects method: On the other hand, you may want to emphasize the effects of quitting a job—perhaps detailing the emotional and financial consequences—in your body paragraphs. In this case, each paragraph would address one effect.

These two cause-effect essay methods answer different questions. Essays that use the focus-on-causes method answer the question, **"Why does something happen?"** Essays that use the focus-on-effects method answer the question, **"What happens when…?"**

ACTIVITY 1 Studying a Cause-Effect Essay

This focus-on-causes essay answers the question, "Why do people lie?" Discuss the Preview Questions with a classmate. Then read the example essay and answer the questions that follow.

Preview Questions

1. Why do you think people lie?

2. Is it ever acceptable to lie? Give examples of acceptable and unacceptable lies.

The Truth Behind Lying

1   Most children are taught the virtue of honesty from fairy tales and other stories. The **celebrated** story of Pinocchio, who begins life as a **puppet**, teaches the importance of telling the truth. Every time Pinocchio lies, his nose grows longer and longer. Another story about the boy who "cried wolf" **exemplifies** how lying led to his losing all of his sheep as well as the trust of his fellow villagers. In the United States, young children learn the tale of young George Washington, who finally admits to his father that he cut down a cherry tree. These types of stories show children that "honesty is the best policy." Still, if this is the case, then why do so many people lie? The fact is that human beings lie for many reasons.

2   One reason for lying has to do with minimizing a mistake. While it is true that everyone makes a **blunder** from time to time, some people do not have the courage to admit their errors because they fear blame. For example, students might lie to their teachers about unfinished homework. They might say that they left the work at home when, in fact, they did not do the work at all. These students do not want to seem irresponsible, so they make up an excuse—a lie—to save face.

celebrated: famous, renowned

a puppet: a toy that is moved by strings

to exemplify: represent, typify

a blunder: a careless mistake

3   Another reason people lie is to get out of situations that they do not want to be in or cannot manage. For example, if a company decides to have a weekend meeting, one of the managers might not feel like attending. She may call her boss and give this excuse: "I've been fighting off a cold all week, and I truly cannot risk getting the others sick. I'll be sure to get all of the notes on Monday." When individuals do not want to admit the truth and then face the consequences, they use lies to **avoid** difficulties.

to avoid: to keep away from

4   In contrast, some people might tell a "white lie" when they do not want to hurt someone else's feelings. For example, if a good friend shows up with an **unflattering** new haircut, one could be truthful and say, "That haircut looks awful. What were you thinking?!" A more likely scenario is to say, "It's very original! It suits you," and spare the friend's feelings. These types of lies are generally not considered negative or wrong. In fact, many people who have told the truth to loved ones, only to see the negative reaction, wish they *had* told a white lie. Therefore, white lies can be useful in maintaining good relationships.

unflattering: unattractive, not favorable

5   A somewhat different reason for lying has to do with self-protection. Parents, particularly those with small children, may teach their children to use this type of "protective" lie in certain circumstances. What should children do if a stranger calls while the parents are out? Many parents teach their children to explain that mom and dad are too busy to come to the phone at that time. In this situation, protective lying can prevent harm or disaster.

6   People lie for many reasons, both good and bad. However, before people **resort to** lying in order to cover up mistakes or to avoid unpleasant situations, perhaps the motives for lying should be analyzed. One's lies may one day be exposed and cause severe embarrassment or the loss of people's trust.

to resort to: to do something only because other options have failed

Post-Reading

1. What is the thesis statement?_____

_____

2. What three examples of liars from famous stories does the author give in the introduction?

    a. _____

    b. _____

    c. _____

3 In Paragraph 4, the idiom *a white lie* is used in the topic sentence but is not defined. Write your own

definition of a white lie. _____

_____

4. In Paragraph 5, the author supports the topic sentence by giving an example of a dangerous situation. What example does the author give?

_____

_____

5. Reread the concluding paragraph of "The Truth Behind Lying." Does the writer offer a suggestion, an

opinion, or a prediction? _____ Write the final sentence here.

_____

_____

ACTIVITY 2 **Studying a Focus-on-Effects Essay**

This focus-on-effects essay discusses some of the effects of the breakup of the Soviet Union. Discuss the Preview Questions with a classmate. Then read the essay and answer the questions that follow.

1. What do you know about the Soviet Union? _____

2. Can you name any countries that were part of the Soviet Union?

_____

_____

The Fall

1   For almost 50 years, the Cold War was one of the most talked about issues in international politics. Tensions between Western countries and the former Soviet Union were high, and the world felt the potential danger of a terrible conflict. When the Iron Curtain fell in 1991, many countries **rejoiced**. Independent-minded Soviet Republics got the independence they had wanted, and the communist **ideology** that had been so **prevalent** began to lose ground. Now, more than two decades after the breakup of the Soviet Union, the effects are still being felt.

to rejoice: to celebrate

an ideology: a system of beliefs

prevalent: common, accepted

2   One of the most obvious changes in post-communist **Eurasia** has been the **shift** to a market economy. Governments that once had **subsidized** the costs of basic necessities, such as food, transportation, housing, and electricity, are now letting competition and external factors determine the prices of these items. Inflation is high, and many citizens are having a difficult time adjusting to the **fluctuations** in prices based on supply and demand. However, imported goods are now commonplace in local markets, so consumers have more choices in what they buy. While the switch to a market economy is often a painful process, a majority of the citizens of the former Soviet Union are still confident that they will benefit financially from the economic changes.

Eurasia: the area of Europe and Asia

a shift: a change

to subsidize: to finance, support

a fluctuation: a movement or change

3   Another anticipated effect of the fall of the Iron Curtain is **sovereignty**. The Soviet Union existed as one entity for many years, but many independent republics emerged, including Estonia, Latvia, Lithuania, Georgia, Ukraine, and Uzbekistan. These republics are currently in the process of shaping their own independent identities. They can focus on rebuilding their own cultures, languages, and priorities. This empowerment increases national pride and uniqueness. The idea of all Soviets being one and the same is certainly no more. Clearly, national identity is at the **forefront** of many people's minds.

sovereignty: self-government, supremacy

the forefront: in the position of most importance, vanguard

4   While many former Soviets now feel a sense of national identity, the fall of the Soviet Union has taken away the identity of others. Many different ethnic groups have lived in this part of the world for generations. They were raised as Soviets, spoke Russian as a native language, and were taught to believe that they were citizens of the great superpower. Koreans, Tartars, Uighurs, and other ethnic groups can be found in most of the former Soviet Republics. Now that independence has spread from Eastern Europe to Central Asia, many of these citizens are considered minority groups. Where their ancestors are from does not matter to them as much as their current homeland. They may look Korean or Chinese, but most of them do not speak those languages and have not had ties with these parts of the world for many years. As the newly formed republics try to **reinvigorate** their traditions and values, many of the ethnic minorities tend to feel left out with no place to really call home.

to reinvigorate: to revitalize, bring back to life

5   The fall of the Soviet Union is perhaps one of the most **momentous** events of the last century. Walls fell, markets opened, and people rejoiced in the streets, anticipating a life filled with opportunities and freedom to make their own choices. A system that took so long to build will probably need as much time, if not more, to truly adapt to the free enterprise system that is now the world model.

momentous: important, eventful

Post-Reading

1. What is the writer's main message in this essay?

   _____

   _____

2. Reread the thesis statement of "The Fall." Is the thesis stated or implied?

   _____

3. **a.** In Paragraph 2, the writer explains that one effect of the Soviet breakup is the new market economy. What examples does the writer give to show that countries are now in a market economy?

   _____

   _____

   b. In Paragraph 4, the author writes about ethnic minorities and their problems. Which minorities are specifically mentioned, and what problems are they having?

   _____

   _____

4. In Paragraph 2, find a word that has approximately the same meaning as the word *shift* and write it

   here. _____

5. Find the boldfaced vocabulary word in the final paragraph of this essay. Write a synonym of that

   word here. _____

Developing a Cause-Effect Essay

In this next section, you will work on cause-effect essays as you make an outline, write supporting information, study connectors, and choose a topic. Practicing these skills will help you write an effective cause-effect essay.

ACTIVITY 3 **Outlining Practice**

Complete the following two outlines with a partner. The first one outlines the causes of bullying behavior (focus-on-causes method), and the second one outlines the effects of bullying on the young people who are being bullied (focus-on-effects method). Use your imagination, knowledge of the topic, and understanding of essay organization. Be sure to pay attention to the thesis statements and use them to help you complete the outlines.

Focus-on-Causes Outline

Topic: The causes of bullying behavior

I. Introduction (Paragraph 1)

    A. Hook: _____

    _____

    B. Thesis statement: Bullying behavior can occur for many reasons, some of which are _____

    _____

    _____

    _____

II. Body

    A. Paragraph 2 (Cause 1) topic sentence: Teens often begin bullying because they want to control those who are weaker than they are.

        1. Bullying gives young people an identity—they become well-known in school.

        2. Bullying makes them feel powerful.

        3. _____

SUPPORT

    B. Paragraph 3 (Cause 2) topic sentence: _____

    _____

        1. In many families, both parents work outside the home.

        2. Parents often do not have time to pay attention to their children's needs.

        3. Parents may not be aware that their children are exhibiting aggressive behavior both inside and outside the home.

SUPPORT

    C. Paragraph 4 (Cause 3) topic sentence: _____

    _____

        1. They use violence as a way of identifying themselves.

        2. They may have emotional problems.

        3. Being known for bad behavior is better than not being known at all.

SUPPORT

III. Conclusion (Paragraph 5) (restated thesis): _____

    _____

    _____

The best way to stop young people from bullying and abusing their peers is to educate the public—including teachers, parents, and other children—that bullying is an absolutely unacceptable behavior. Only then will there be a decrease in the number of bullying incidents in school.

Focus-on-Effects Outline

Topic: The effects of bullying on the victim

  I. Introduction (Paragraph 1)

    A. Hook: _____

    _____

    B. Thesis statement: When young people bully others, the effects felt by the weaker student can lead to serious, even deadly, consequences.

  II. Body

    A. Paragraph 2 (Effect 1) topic sentence: Students who are bullied tend to withdraw from society.

      1. They often stop communicating with parents and friends.

      2. They want to hide this embarrassing situation, which can lead to lying.

      3. _____

SUPPORT

33

B. Paragraph 3 (Effect 2) topic sentence: _____

_____

SUPPORT

1. Students lose self-esteem and start questioning their own personalities, thinking that maybe they deserve this bad treatment.

2. They may start focusing only on the bully.

3. Their outlook on life may become darker and darker as the bullying continues.

C. Paragraph 4 (Effect 3) topic sentence: If teens become damaged by the bullying, they may do almost anything to get out of the situation.

SUPPORT

1. They may try to escape from their painful reality by engaging in dangerous activities.

2. They might think about a plan of revenge.

3. _____

III. Conclusion (Paragraph 5) (restated thesis): _____

_____

When young people are victims of bullies, there is a strong chance that they will suffer many negative consequences, not only from the bullies themselves but also as they begin to separate from society. For so many years, bullying was considered a normal part of growing up. However, with the increase of teen anguish due to bullying and the millions of dollars spent on long-term therapy, one has to wonder if bullying should be considered a "normal" activity. In order to ensure a stable and healthy society, individuals need to take a harder look at this negative behavior that hurts not only the bullied child and the bully, but the family and society as a whole.

ACTIVITY 4 **Supporting Information**

The cause-effect essay on the next page is missing the supporting information. As you read the essay, work with a partner to write supporting sentences for each paragraph. If you need more space, use a separate piece of paper. After you finish, compare your supporting information with that of other students.

Television at Its Worst

1   Mr. Stevenson has just come home from a terribly tiring day at work. The first thing he does, after taking off his tie and shoes, is plop down on the couch and turn on the television. Does this sound like a normal routine? It should, because Mr. Stevenson's actions are repeated by millions around the world. People use television to relax and to forget about their daily troubles. However, what started out decades ago as an exciting, new type of family entertainment is currently being blamed for serious problems, especially in children. Many researchers now claim that too much television is not good for kids. They have a point; watching too much TV often does have negative effects on children and adolescents.

2   One negative effect of TV on kids is laziness. _____

_____

_____

_____

_____

_____

3   Another problem with TV watching and kids is that children may have difficulty distinguishing between what is real and what is not. _____

_____

_____

_____

_____

_____

4   Finally, television may lead children to _____

_____

_____

_____

_____

_____

5   Television has changed over the years to include more and more programs that are inappropriate for children. For TV to once again play a more positive role in children's lives, something must be done. Society cannot just continue to wonder why children are behaving poorly. It is time to change TV viewing behavior.

Grammar for Writing

Connectors for Cause-Effect Essays

Connectors show relationships between ideas in sentences and paragraphs. In cause-effect essays, writers commonly use the connecting words and phrases in the following charts.

Connectors That Show Cause

To Introduce Sentences	Examples
As a result of + Noun, Subject + Verb.	**As a result of the rain**, we all got wet.
Because of + Noun, Subject + Verb.	**Because of** the rain, we all got wet.
Due to + Noun, Subject + Verb.	**Due to** the rain, we all got wet.
As Part of an Adverb Clause	**Examples**
Because + Subject + Verb, Subject + Verb.	**Because** it rained, we all got wet.
Since + Subject + Verb, Subject + Verb.	**Since** it rained, we all got wet.

Connectors That Show Effect

Between Sentences	Examples
For this reason, Subject + Verb.	Out of the blue, it started to rain heavily and none of us was prepared for it. **For this reason,** we all got wet.
Therefore, Subject + Verb.	**Therefore,** we all got wet.
As a result, Subject + Verb.	**As a result,** we all got wet.
Thus, Subject + Verb.	**Thus,** we all got wet.
Consequently, Subject + Verb.	**Consequently,** we all got wet.

For a more complete list of connectors, see the *Brief Writer's Handbook*, pages 120–121.

ACTIVITY 5 **Connectors**

Read the next essay (focus-on-effects method) and underline the appropriate connector in each set of parentheses. Refer to the charts above, if necessary.

Effects of Studying Abroad

1   Globalization has impacted all aspects of modern-day life, from a country's commerce and politics to a family's everyday decision-making strategy at the grocery store. One of the elements of globalization that is of particular interest in the field of education is study abroad programs. Host countries and institutions are eager to accept international students while the students are intrigued by the possibility of international travel. Studying abroad has become an opportunity that is available to many students, especially those at the university level. Certainly, studying abroad is not for everyone; (however / as a result), for those students who experience it, the positive effects will stay with them forever.

2   One important effect of studying abroad is a student's greater understanding of a different educational system. The curriculum, **availability** and types of lectures, and the educational environment as a whole will differ from that of the student's home country. At first the student may be confused, but this **exposure** to a different curriculum will broaden his or her educational horizons **in the long run**. (For this reason / As a result of) the new academic culture, the student will be able to better appreciate his or her own educational setting later at home.

the availability: accessibility, ease of use

the exposure: experience with, introduction to

in the long run: in time, ultimately

3   Individuals who study abroad also develop their understanding of a different popular culture. Even if the host country's language is the same, there are many cultural experiences that the student will have. From learning how to live with a host family to finding the least expensive grocery store, the student will come across new and sometimes **frustrating** customs and **conventions**. (Since / Consequently), he or she will need to adapt to rules and behaviors that are unfamiliar. The comfortable, well-known lifestyle of the student's past has disappeared and been replaced with the newness of everything. This life exercise may be difficult in the beginning of the study abroad period, but it becomes easier as time passes and the student develops a better understanding of the host country.

frustrating: annoying, difficult, exasperating

a convention: rule

4   Finally, studying abroad gives students the opportunity to serve as ambassadors for their home countries. A foreign student on a university campus can be an uncommon sight. The host institution, including the local **student body**, will form an impression of the student's culture based on interactions with him or her. (As a result / Due to), the student should remember to represent his or her country and culture in the best possible light.

the student body: student population at a particular school

5   To summarize, there are a number of effects of studying abroad, not only for the student but also for the host institution. While some of the experiences may seem difficult at the time, the long-term effects can be considered positive. This is in large part (because of / because) globalization in the education **sector**.

a sector: area, part

Grammar for Writing

Noun Clauses

Noun clauses take the place of a noun or a noun phrase in a sentence. Study the following chart:

Function	Noun **Phrase**	Noun **Clause**
Subject	**The pizza** was delicious.	**What I ate for dinner** was delicious.
Object	I don't know **the answer**.	I don't know **what the answer is**.
Object of preposition	No one is interested in **his remarks**.	No one is interested in **what he said**.
Subject complement	The main problem is **a lack of workers**.	The main problem is **that there are not enough workers**.

Noun clauses begin with the following connectors:

Adverbial Connector	*Wh-* Connectors	*Wh*-ever Connectors
if	how, what, when, where,	whatever, whenever, wherever,
that	which, who, whom,	whichever, whoever, whomever
whether	whose, why	

ACTIVITY 6 Identifying Noun Clauses and Adjective Clauses

The following sentences were taken from this unit. Each sentence contains either a noun clause or an adjective clause. Underline the clause (beginning with a connector) in each sentence and identify it as either a noun clause (NC) or an adjective clause (AC).

_____ 1. A system that took so long to build will probably need as much time, if not more, to truly adapt to the free enterprise system.

_____ 2. Another problem with TV watching and kids is that children may have difficulty distinguishing between reality and fantasy.

_____ 3. Governments that once had subsidized the costs of basic necessities are now letting competition and external factors determine the prices of these items.

_____ 4. In fact, many people who have told the truth to loved ones, only to see the negative reaction, wish they *had* told a white lie.

_____ 5. It is true that everyone makes a blunder from time to time.

_____ 6. Parents may not be aware that their children are exhibiting aggressive behavior both inside and outside the home.

_____ 7. Society cannot just continue to wonder why children are behaving poorly.

_____ 8. These types of stories typically show children that "honesty is the best policy."

_____ 9. What started out decades ago as an exciting type of family entertainment is currently being blamed for problems, especially in children.

_____10. Where their ancestors are from does not matter to them as much as their current homeland.

Choosing Words Carefully

In all writing, including cause-effect essays, attention to precise language is important. Wordiness, or using unnecessary words, is a common problem for many writers. If you can eliminate wordiness from your writing, your essays will be clearer and easier to read.

Wordiness

Some writers think that the more words they use, the better an essay will sound. However, in academic writing in English, it is important to be as concise as possible. Unnecessary words and phrases do not improve your writing. Instead, they make it hard for readers to understand what you want to say.

The list on the left contains common **wordy** phrases. Good writers use the fewest words possible to make a point. In other words, they are being **concise**. Try to avoid using the phrases on the left; substitute them with the phrases on the right.

Wordy	Concise
at that point in time	at that time
despite the fact that + Subject + Verb	despite + Noun
for all intents and purposes	Ø—use nothing
for the purpose of	for
in my opinion, I believe…	in my opinion… *or* I believe…
in the event that	if
in the final analysis	finally
in the vicinity of	near
it goes without saying	Ø—use nothing
it seems unnecessary to point out	Ø—use nothing
made a statement saying	said
the reason why is	because
when all is said and done	Ø—use nothing

ACTIVITY 7 Wordiness

The introductory paragraph on the next page is from a cause-effect essay, and it contains seven examples of wordy phrases. Underline them as you find them. Then, on a separate piece of paper, rewrite the paragraph without the wordy phrases and make it more concise. Note: There is more than one correct way of rewriting this paragraph.

Fat-Free Food

In my opinion, I believe that the fat-free food industry is a tremendous money-making business. In fact, recent research has shown that fat-free products are considered only a minor prescription for the purpose of losing weight. Nutritionists have made statements saying that, for all intents and purposes, more important steps to losing weight are exercising and eating well-balanced meals. Despite the fact that this information has appeared, many people still seem to believe that, when all is said and done, eating fat-free food is the best dieting method. The content of the following essay shows some interesting reasons for this fat-free phenomenon.

Redundancy

Redundancy—a kind of wordiness—is the unnecessary repetition of information. When you write, you may want to impress your readers with an eloquent essay that is full of thought-provoking information. One way that writers often try to do this is by loading up on information. You may think, "The more information I have in my essay, the more my readers will enjoy it." This is not usually the case, especially if, instead of adding information, you repeat what you have already said. Repetition can occur in the wording of short phrases as well as in sentences.

Redundant phrases. The list on the left contains commonly used redundant phrases. Try to avoid them in your writing. (If you are not sure why the phrases are redundant, look up the meanings of the two words.)

Change	To
collaborate together	collaborate
completely unanimous	unanimous
courthouse building	courthouse
descend downward	descend
erupt violently	erupt
exactly identical	identical
free gift	gift
loud explosion	explosion
merge together	merge
repeat again	repeat
unexpected surprise	surprise

Look at the example sentences below. The first sentence contains the same information as the second sentence.

Redundant Sentence The United States is the most influential power in the world. Partly because of its abundant material resources and stable political system, this country has great influence in global affairs.

Concise Sentence The United States has a great influence in global affairs in part because of its abundant material resources and stable political system.

Underline the redundant information in this paragraph. Then compare your work with a partner's.

Paragraph 2

Extrasensory Perception

Many people love to watch science-fiction stories on TV or at the movies. TV shows and films, such as *Star Trek,* are popular not only because they creatively show how future life might be in 300 years, but also because they introduce us to characters from other worlds, planets, and galaxies. Perhaps one of the most popular kinds of characters in these futuristic programs is a person with ESP, or extrasensory perception. ESP is a sense that allows one person to read the mind of another without the exchange of words. These characters, who can read minds and know the innermost thoughts and secrets of other people, often use their gift in less than noble ways. One must remember, however, that these scenes take place in an untrue and fictitious situation. A more interesting concept is to think about what would really happen if ordinary, everyday people possessed ESP.

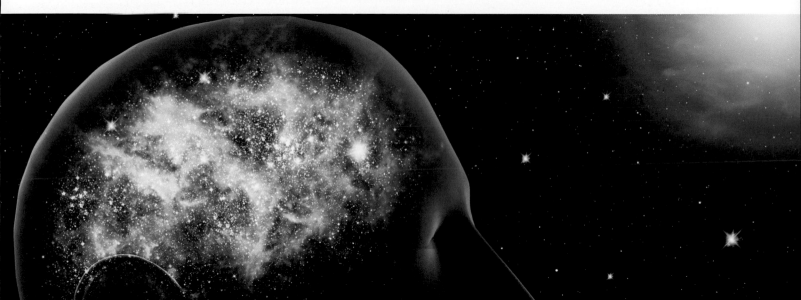

Building Better Vocabulary

ACTIVITY 9 **Word Associations**

Circle the word or phrase that is most closely related to the word or phrase on the left. If necessary, use a dictionary to check the meaning of words you do not know.

	A	**B**
1. shift	moving	unmoving
2. an ideology	beliefs	smart
3. momentous	for a short time	important
4. fluctuation	stable	unstable
5. abroad	inside the country	overseas
6. to rejoice	happy feelings	sad feelings
7. the forefront	new ideas	old ideas
8. availability	presence	thought
9. exposure	hidden	open
10. a blunder	a mistake	an opinion

ACTIVITY 10 **Using Collocations**

Fill in each blank with the word or phrase on the left that most naturally completes the phrase on the right. If necessary, use a dictionary to check the meaning of words you do not know.

1. lunch / time	to have a difficult _____
2. on / to	one negative effect of TV _____ people
3. out of / up to	to get _____ a bad situation
4. by / for	convenient _____ everyone
5. run / time	in the long _____
6. play / run	to _____ a role
7. in / of	effects _____ studying abroad
8. part / step	a normal _____ of life
9. for / to	to resort _____ an alternative plan
10. in / to	children tend _____ be active

Developing Ideas for Writing

Many writers can think of good topics, but they have trouble developing their topics into essays. One brainstorming method that helps is to ask questions about the topic—*Who? What? Where? When? Why? How?* This process often leads to new ideas that can be used in an essay. Especially for a cause-effect essay, good writers ask the question *Why?*

ACTIVITY 11 Starting with Questions

The following questions can all be developed into cause-effect essays. Try to give at least three answers to each question.

1. Why do people gain too much weight?

   _____

   _____

   _____

2. What usually happens after a natural disaster?

   _____

   _____

   _____

3. Why do people quit their jobs?

   _____

   _____

   _____

4. What would happen if the world's biggest economies failed?

   _____

   _____

   _____

5. Why are more and more people studying a second (or third) language?

   _____

   _____

   _____

6. What are the effects of playing a team sport?

   _____

   _____

   _____

7. What are the causes of _____? (Think of your own topic.)

_____

_____

8. What are the effects of _____? (Think of your own topic.)

_____

_____

Brainstorming

In the next activity, you will use a brainstorming technique called **clustering**. Here is an example of clustering; the topic is the effects of ozone depletion on the environment.

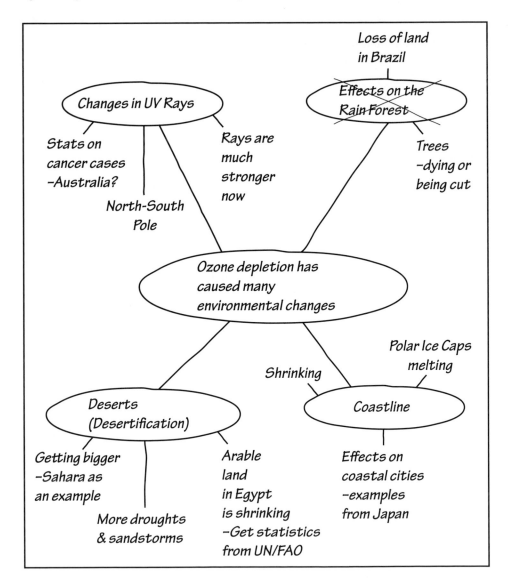

Original Student Writing: Cause-Effect Essay

ACTIVITY 12 **Clustering Ideas**

Choose a topic from Activity 11. Brainstorm some ideas about your topic using the clustering method. Write all your ideas. When you have finished, cross out the ideas that you do not like or do not want to include in your essay. Explain your brainstorming cluster to a classmate.

ACTIVITY 13 **Planning with an Outline**

Complete the outline below as a guide to help you brainstorm a more detailed plan for your cause-effect essay. Use your ideas from Activity 12. You may need to use either more or fewer points under each heading. Write in complete sentences where possible.

Topic: _____

  I. Introduction (Paragraph 1)

    A. Hook: _____

    B. Connecting information: _____

      _____

    C. Thesis statement: _____

      _____

 II. Body

    A. Paragraph 2 (first cause or effect) topic sentence: _____

      _____

        1. _____

    SUPPORT **2.** _____

        3. _____

    B. Paragraph 3 (second cause or effect) topic sentence: _____

      _____

        1. _____

    SUPPORT **2.** _____

        3. _____

C. Paragraph 4 (third cause or effect) topic sentence: _____

_____

SUPPORT

1. _____

2. _____

3. _____

III. Conclusion (paragraph 5)

  A. Restated thesis: _____

_____

  B. Suggestion, opinion, or prediction: _____

_____

Writer's Note

Personal Writing Style

Some writers work well from a detailed outline, and some can write well from a general outline. Some writers write the introduction first, and some write it last. Writing is an individual activity. Use the guidelines in this book and follow the process that works best for you.

ACTIVITY 14 **Peer Editing Your Outline**

Exchange books with a partner and look at Activity 13. Read your partner's outline. Then use Peer Editing Sheet 1 on ELTNGL.com/sites/els to help you comment on your partner's outline. Use your partner's feedback to revise your outline. Make sure you have enough information to develop your supporting sentences.

ACTIVITY 15 **Writing a Cause-Effect Essay**

Write a cause-effect essay based on your revised outline from Activity 14. Use at least two of the vocabulary words or phrases presented in Activities 9 and 10. Underline these words and phrases in your essay. Be sure to refer to the seven steps in the writing process in the *Brief Writer's Handbook* on pages 96–102.

If you need ideas for words and phrases, see the Useful Vocabulary for Better Writing on pages 121–124.

ACTIVITY 16 **Peer Editing Your Essay**

Exchange papers from Activity 15 with a partner. Read your partner's essay. Then use Peer Editing Sheet 2 on ELTNGL.com/sites/els to help you comment on your partner's writing. Be sure to offer positive suggestions and comments that will help your partner improve his or her essay. Consider your partner's comments as you revise your own essay.

Additional Topics for Writing

Here are more ideas for topics for a cause-effect essay. Before you write, be sure to refer to the seven steps in the writing process in the *Brief Writer's Handbook*, on pages 96–102.

PHOTO
TOPIC: Look at the photograph on pages 24–25. As climates change, many parts of the world are experiencing extreme weather such as heavy rains or snow, intense heat without any rain, and powerful storms. What are some effects of extreme weather?

TOPIC 2: Going to college is a dream for many people. Some do the work, graduate, and find good jobs. Other students, however, never finish their university studies. Write an essay about what causes students to drop out of college.

TOPIC 3: Friendships are an integral part of a person's life. Unfortunately, some of these relationships do not last. Write an essay highlighting some of the reasons that friendships sometimes die.

TOPIC 4: Many people enjoy traveling and experiencing other cultures. What are some of the beneficial effects of international travel on an individual?

TOPIC 5: Children are learning to use computers at a very early age. What are some effects (positive or negative) that computers can have on the intellectual development of children?

Timed Writing

How quickly can you write in English? There are many times when you must write quickly such as on a test. It is important to feel comfortable during those times. Timed-writing practice can make you feel better about writing quickly in English.

1. Take out a piece of paper.

2. Read the essay guidelines and the writing prompt.

3. Write a basic outline, including the thesis and your three main points.

4. Write a five-paragraph essay.

5. You have 40 minutes to write your essay.

Cause-Effect Essay Guidelines

- Use the focus-on-causes method.

- Remember to give your essay a title.

- Double-space your essay.

- Write as legibly as possible (if you are not using a computer).

- Select an appropriate principle of organization for your topic.

- Include a short introduction (with a thesis statement), three body paragraphs, and a conclusion.

- Try to give yourself a few minutes before the end of the activity to review your work. Check for spelling, verb tense, and subject-verb agreement mistakes.

Why do people keep pets?

NOTES

CHANGING THE PLANET 3

A residential suburb in
Arizona, United States

A Look at the maps and answer the questions.

1. What four types of human impact does the main map show?

2. Which regions experience the most deforestation, desertification, and pollution?

3. What are some causes of air pollution, deforestation, and desertification?

B Match the correct form of the words in blue to their definitions.

_____ (n) the layer of gases around a planet

_____ (n) a substance used by farmers to help crops grow

_____ (n) gradual destruction by natural causes such as the weather, the sea, and rivers

Deforestation

Loss of forest cover contributes to a buildup of carbon dioxide (a greenhouse gas) in the **atmosphere**. It also causes soil **erosion** and a loss of soil nutrients.

THE HUMAN IMPACT

Around the world, natural environments are under pressure from the release of air and water pollutants, and by the removal of vegetation to extract mineral resources or to create land for farming.

In more developed countries, industries create waste and pollution; farmers use **fertilizers** and pesticides that run off into water supplies; and motor vehicles release exhaust fumes into the air.

In less developed countries, forests are cut down for fuel or to clear land for farming; grasslands are turned into deserts as farmers and herders overuse the land; and expanding urban areas face problems of water quality and sanitation.

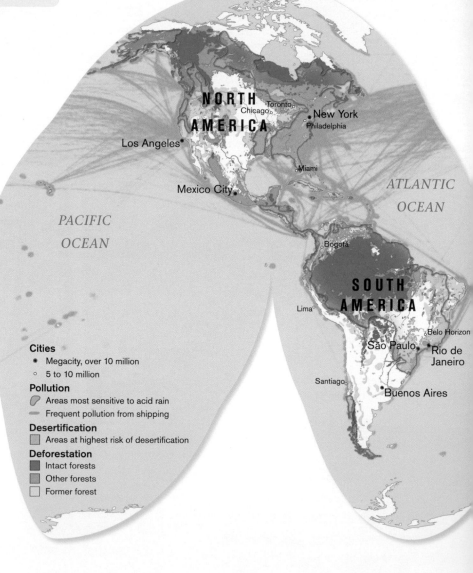

Cities
- ● Megacity, over 10 million
- ○ 5 to 10 million

Pollution
- Areas most sensitive to acid rain
- Frequent pollution from shipping

Desertification
- Areas at highest risk of desertification

Deforestation
- Intact forests
- Other forests
- Former forest

Desertification

In semiarid and arid areas—which receive limited rainfall—land that is overgrazed or overcultivated can become desertlike.

Pollution

Poor air quality is a serious environmental problem in many parts of the world. Smoke from industrial plants may contain particles that contribute to acid rain.

The map below uses population density, land use, transportation, and energy production and use to identify areas of Earth where human impact is greatest.

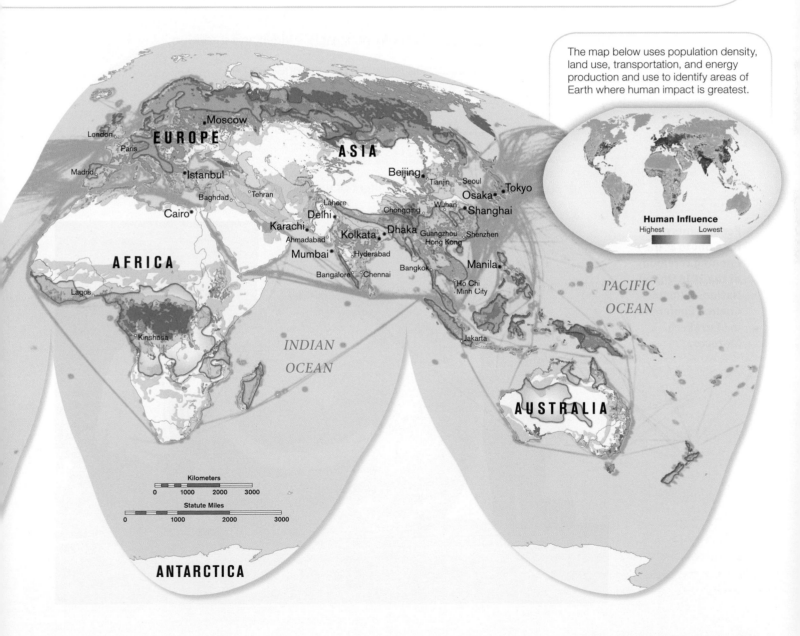

Human Influence
Highest — Lowest

Reading

PREPARING TO READ

BUILDING
VOCABULARY

A The words in **blue** below are used in the reading passage. Match the correct form of each word to its definition.

Diplomats and scientists from around the world met to discuss climate issues at the 2016 United Nations Climate Change Conference in Marrakech, Morocco. The conference was **devoted to** discussing the reduction of global carbon emissions, which contribute to global warming. The dominant **perspective** on global warming is that it is a **consequence** of human activities. A **dramatic** increase in carbon emissions in the last several years has had a **profound** effect on the global climate. While most experts agree that it is impossible to completely **eliminate** carbon emissions, they do believe it is possible to cool down the planet.

1. _____ (adj) very noticeable; sudden and surprising

2. _____ (adj) focused only on one thing

3. _____ (v) to remove completely

4. _____ (n) a way of thinking about something

5. _____ (adj) very great

6. _____ (n) the effect or result of an action

▶ **Participants pose for a photo at the opening ceremony of the 2016 United Nations Climate Change Conference in Marrakech, Morocco.**

B Complete the sentences with the words in the box. Use a dictionary to help you.

| concept | criteria | current | essentially | satisfy | transform |

1. One of the _____ for naming a new animal species is that the name must be easy to remember.

2. A basic scientific _____ is cause and effect: the idea that an event is caused by or affected by another event.

3. Coal is _____ the remains of prehistoric plants. Over time, physical and chemical changes _____ ancient plant material into a substance that could be used as fuel.

4. Most animal species _____ the basic needs of their young until their offspring reach a certain age and can take care of themselves.

5. If our _____ efforts to lower carbon emissions are not significant enough to stop climate change, global warming may become worse in the future.

C Note answers to the questions below. Then discuss with a partner.

1. What are some of the **consequences** of human existence on the planet?

_____

2. What do you think is the most **dramatic** consequence?

_____

3. What are some **current** efforts to deal with these consequences?

_____

D How do we know what Earth was like in the past? How do we know about plants or animals that existed in the past? Note your ideas below. Then discuss with a partner.

_____

_____

E Look at the photos and infographics in the reading and read the captions. Read the title and the first sentence of each paragraph. Circle your answers to the questions.

1. What do you think this reading is about? Circle your answer (a–c).

   It's an explanation of how _____ on the planet is changing the way people in the future might describe the current geological period.

   a. the effect of global warming
   b. the overall human impact
   c. the increasing population

2. What time period do you think *Anthropocene* describes?

   a. an ancient period   b. the current period   c. a future period

3. What area of science is this passage mainly about?

   a. biology   b. climatology   c. geology

THE HUMAN AGE

by Elizabeth Kolbert

Western Minnesota: Vast wheat fields and long train lines have created a distinctive human landscape in the Midwestern United States.

> Human beings have altered the planet so much in just the past century or two that we now have a new name for a new epoch: the Anthropocene.

🎧 Track 3

A **The word** *Anthropocene* was coined by Dutch chemist Paul Crutzen in 2002. Crutzen, who shared a Nobel Prize for discovering the effects of ozone-depleting compounds, was sitting at a scientific conference one day. The conference chairman kept referring to the Holocene, the epoch that began 11,500 years ago, at the end of the last ice age, and that—officially, at least—continues to this day.

B "Let's stop it," Crutzen recalls blurting out. "We are no longer in the Holocene. We are in the Anthropocene." It was quiet in the room for a while. When the group took a coffee break, the Anthropocene was the main topic of conversation.

C Way back in the 1870s, an Italian geologist named Antonio Stoppani proposed that people had introduced a new era, which he labeled the Anthropozoic. Stoppani's proposal was ignored; other scientists found it unscientific. The Anthropocene, by contrast, struck a chord. The human impact on the world has become a lot more obvious since Stoppani's day, in part because the size of the population has roughly quadrupled,[1] to nearly seven billion.

D When Crutzen wrote up the Anthropocene idea in the journal *Nature*, the **concept** was immediately picked up by researchers working in a wide range of disciplines. Soon, it began to appear regularly in the scientific press. At first, most of the scientists using the new geologic term were not geologists. Jan Zalasiewicz, a British geologist, found the discussions intriguing. "I noticed that Crutzen's term was appearing in the serious literature, without quotation marks and without a sense of irony," he says.

E In 2007, Zalasiewicz was serving as chairman of the Geological Society of London's Stratigraphy[2] Commission. At a meeting, he decided to ask his fellow stratigraphers what they thought of the Anthropocene. Twenty-one of twenty-two thought the concept had merit. The group agreed to look at it as a formal problem in geology. Would the Anthropocene **satisfy** the **criteria** used for naming a new epoch?

F The rock record of the present doesn't exist yet, of course. So the question was: When it does, will human impacts show up as "stratigraphically significant"? The answer, Zalasiewicz's group decided, is yes—though not necessarily for the reasons you would expect.

---

[1]If something **quadruples**, it increases by a factor of four.
[2]**Stratigraphy** is a branch of geology concerned with the study of rock layers.

Earth's Geological Timeline

start of the Anthropocene?

Era	Period		Epoch	Millions of Years
Cenozoic	Quaternary		Holocene	
			Pleistocene	1.5
	Neogene		Pliocene	
			Miocene	2.3
	Paleogene		Oligocene	
			Eocene	
			Paleocene	65
Mesozoic	Cretaceous			
	Jurassic			
	Triassic			250
Paleozoic	Permian			
	Carboniferous	Pennsylvanian		
		Mississippian		
	Devonian			
	Silurian			
	Ordovician			
	Cambrian			540
Precambrian	Proterozoic			2500
	Archean			3800
	Hadean			4600

In geology, epochs are relatively short time spans, though they can extend for tens of millions of years. Periods, such as the Ordovician and the Cretaceous, last much longer, and eras, like the Mesozoic, longer still. The boundaries between epochs are defined by changes preserved in sedimentary rocks[3] —for example, the emergence of one type of commonly fossilized organism, or the disappearance of another.

PROBABLY THE MOST OBVIOUS way humans are altering the planet is by building cities, which are **essentially** vast stretches of man-made materials—steel, glass, concrete, and brick. But it turns out most cities are not good candidates for long-term preservation: they're built on land, and on land the forces of **erosion** tend to win out over those of sedimentation. From a geologic **perspective**, the most plainly visible human effects on the landscape today "may in some ways be the most transient,[4]" Zalasiewicz observes.

Humans have also **transformed** the world through farming; something like 38 percent of the planet's ice-free land is now **devoted to** agriculture. Here again, some of the effects that seem most significant today—runoff from the use of **fertilizers** on fields, for example—will leave behind only subtle traces at best. Future geologists are most likely to grasp the scale of 21st-century industrial agriculture from the pollen[5] record—from the monochrome[6] stretches of corn, wheat, and soy pollen that will have replaced the varied record left behind by rain forests or prairies.

G

H

[3] **Sedimentary rocks** are formed from sediment—solid material that settles at the bottom of a liquid.
[4] **Transient** describes a situation that lasts only a short time or is constantly changing.
[5] **Pollen** is a powder produced by flowers that fertilizes other flowers of the same species.
[6] If something is **monochrome**, it is all one color.

The leveling of the world's forests will send at least two coded signals to future stratigraphers, though deciphering the first may be tricky. Massive soil erosion is causing increasing sedimentation[7] in some parts of the world—but at the same time, the dams we've built on most of the world's major rivers are holding back sediment that would otherwise be washed to sea. The second signal of deforestation should come through clearer. Loss of forest habitat is a major cause of extinctions, which are now happening at a rate hundreds or even thousands of times higher than during most of the past half billion years. If **current** trends continue, the rate may soon be tens of thousands of times higher.

Probably the most significant change, from a geologic perspective, is one that's invisible to us— the change in the composition of the **atmosphere**. Carbon dioxide emissions are colorless, odorless, and—in an immediate sense—harmless. But their warming effects could easily push global temperatures to levels that have not been seen for millions of years. Some plants and animals are already shifting their ranges toward the Poles, and those shifts will leave traces in the fossil record. Some species will not survive the warming at all. Meanwhile, rising temperatures could eventually raise sea levels 20 feet or more.

Long after our cars, cities, and factories have turned to dust, the **consequences** of burning billions of tons' worth of coal and oil are likely to be clearly discernible. As carbon dioxide warms the planet, it also seeps into the oceans and acidifies them. Sometime this century, they may become acidified to the point that corals can no longer construct reefs, which would register in the geologic record as a "reef gap." Reef gaps have marked each of the past five major mass extinctions. The most recent one—which is believed to have been caused by the impact of an asteroid—took place 65 million years ago, at the end of the Cretaceous period; it **eliminated** not just the dinosaurs but also the plesiosaurs, pterosaurs, and ammonites.[8] Since then, there has been nothing to match the scale of the changes that we are now seeing in our oceans. To future geologists, Zalasiewicz says, our impact may look as sudden and **profound** as that of an asteroid.

---

[7] **Sedimentation** is the process by which solid material—especially earth and pieces of rock—settles at the bottom of a liquid.
[8] **Plesiosaurs**, **pterosaurs**, and **ammonites** are extinct prehistoric organisms.

Colorado River Delta, Mexico: Aerial photography can illustrate the human impact on Earth's landscape.

> " Do we decide the Anthropocene's here, or do we wait 20 years and things will be even worse? "

IF WE HAVE INDEED entered a new epoch, then when exactly did it begin? When did human impacts rise to the level of geologic significance?

William Ruddiman, a paleoclimatologist at the University of Virginia, has proposed that the invention of agriculture some 8,000 years ago—and the deforestation that resulted—led to an increase in atmospheric CO_2 just large enough to stave off what otherwise would have been the start of a new ice age. In his view, humans have

Trotternish, Isle of Skye: Millions of years of history are recorded in the rocks of Scotland. Are we creating a new chapter in Earth's geological history?

been the dominant force on the planet practically since the start of the Holocene. Crutzen has suggested that the Anthropocene began in the late 18th century, when, ice cores show, carbon dioxide levels began what has since proved to be an uninterrupted rise. Other scientists put the beginning of the new epoch in the middle of the 20th century, when the rates of both population growth and consumption accelerated rapidly.

Zalasiewicz now heads a working group of the International Commission on Stratigraphy (ICS) that is tasked with officially determining whether the Anthropocene deserves to be incorporated into the geologic timescale. A final decision will require votes by both the ICS and its parent organization, the International Union of Geological Sciences. The process is likely to take years. As it drags on, the decision may well become easier. Some scientists argue that we've not yet reached the start of the Anthropocene—not because we haven't had a **dramatic** impact on the planet, but because the next several decades are likely to prove even more stratigraphically significant than the past few centuries. "Do we decide the Anthropocene's here, or do we wait 20 years and things will be even worse?" says Mark Williams, a geologist and colleague of Zalasiewicz's at the University of Leicester in England.

Crutzen, who started the debate, thinks its real value won't lie in revisions to geology textbooks. His purpose is broader: He wants to focus our attention on the consequences of our collective action—and on how we might still avert the worst. "What I hope," he says, "is that the term *Anthropocene* will be a warning to the world."

Adapted from "The Age of Man," by Elizabeth Kolbert: National Geographic Magazine, March 2011

National Magazine Award winner Elizabeth Kolbert has written extensively about environmental issues for *National Geographic Magazine, The New Yorker,* and other publications. Her book *The Sixth Extinction* won the 2015 Pulitzer Prize for general nonfiction.

UNDERSTANDING THE READING

A Note answers to the questions below.

1. What is the purpose of Kolbert's article? Complete the main idea.

    Kolbert's purpose is to present the idea of a new _____ and to show how our human impact will be noted in the future.

2. What does "Anthropocene" mean? Explain it in your own words.

    _____

    _____

3. What four main areas does Kolbert examine for signs of human impact?

    cities, _____

B The reading passage has three main parts. Where could you place each of these section heads? Write paragraph letters: **A**, **G**, and **L**.

Section Head	Before Paragraph ...
How We Are Changing the Planet	_____
Tracing the Origins of the Anthropocene	_____
A New Perspective on Earth's History	_____

C Note answers to the questions below. Then discuss with a partner.

1. When was the idea of a new era first proposed? What was it called? Why did people not take it seriously?

    _____

    _____

    _____

2. Why did Crutzen's ideas gain more support than Stoppani's?

    _____

    _____

    _____

3. What are two effects of cutting down forests?

    _____

    _____

    _____

4. How does climate change affect plants and animals? How is it affecting the oceans?

    _____

    _____

    _____

    _____

D Complete the chart summarizing the human impact on our planet. Then discuss this question in a small group: Of the four kinds of human impact, which do you think will leave the most obvious record in the future? Why?

	The Human Impact	Will It Leave a Trace? Why, or Why Not?
Cities	building structures made of ¹_____	No—structures built on land; ²_____ may make them disappear
Farming	farming ³_____ percent of the available land	⁴_____—but only from the ⁵_____ record of the shift from a variety of plants to a few types
Forests	⁶_____ trees	Maybe—sedimentation and ⁷_____ may be noticed
Atmosphere	⁸_____ the atmosphere	Most likely—shifts in habitat range will leave traces in ⁹_____; the world's ¹⁰_____ will become acidified and coral will no longer be able to construct reefs

E Look at the timeline on page 56 and note answers to the questions below. Then discuss your ideas with a partner.

1. What era, period, and epoch are we currently living in?

   Era: _____   Period: _____

   Epoch: _____ or _____

2. When did the current era begin?

   _____

3. How do scientists decide when one epoch ends and another one begins?

   _____

   _____

The acidification of the ocean, caused by high levels of carbon dioxide in the atmosphere, could cause coral reefs to die out.

CRITICAL THINKING:
ANALYZING EVIDENCE

F In the reading passage, what evidence does the writer present in support of either side of the main argument? Take notes in the chart. Then discuss answers to the questions below with a partner.

Argument: Humans are having such a great impact on the planet that the Holocene epoch is over, and we are now living in a new epoch: the Anthropocene.	
Evidence For	Evidence Against

1. Is the evidence on both sides balanced, or is there more evidence for one side than the other?
2. Do the facts and opinions come from reliable sources? Is the information relevant and up to date?

CRITICAL THINKING:
GUESSING MEANING
FROM CONTEXT

G Find and underline the following words and expressions in the reading passage. Use context to guess their meanings. Then match the sentence parts.

1. Para A: If a word is **coined by** someone, ____
2. Para C: If an idea **struck a chord**, ____
3. Para I: If you **decipher** something, ____
4. Para K: If a consequence is **discernible**, ____
5. Para M: If you **stave off** an event, ____
6. Para N: When something **drags on**, ____

a. it continues for a long time.
b. you can detect it.
c. you figure out the meaning of it.
d. you prevent it from happening.
e. it was invented by that person.
f. other people thought it sounded logical.

DEVELOPING READING SKILLS

Cohesion refers to the way that ideas are linked in a text. Writers use certain techniques (sometimes called "cohesive devices") to refer to ideas mentioned elsewhere in the passage. Some of these techniques include pronouns (*one*[s], *another*, *the other*), demonstratives (*this, that, these, those*), and synonyms.

Look at these examples from "The Human Age."

> In 2002, when Crutzen wrote up the Anthropocene idea in the journal Nature, the concept was immediately picked up by researchers working in a wide range of disciplines.

The writer uses a synonym, *the concept*, to refer to *the idea* in the first part of the sentence.

> Wilson calculates that human biomass is already a hundred times larger than that of any other large animal species that has ever walked the Earth.

In this example, the writer uses *that* to refer to *biomass*.

Note: The referent—the word or idea that is referred to—is not always close to the cohesive device. It may be in a different part of the sentence, or in a different sentence or section of the text.

A Circle the word or idea that each underlined word in these extracts refers to.　　　ANALYZING

1. Paragraph D: When Crutzen wrote up the Anthropocene idea in the journal *Nature*, the concept was immediately picked up by researchers working in a wide range of disciplines. Soon, <u>it</u> began to appear regularly in the scientific press.

   a. the researchers　　b. the journal　　　c. the concept

2. Paragraph G: But it turns out most cities are not good candidates for long-term preservation for the simple reason that they're built on land, and on land the forces of erosion tend to win out over <u>those</u> of sedimentation.

   a. forces　　　　b. cities　　　c. candidates

B Find the following excerpts in "The Human Age." Write the words or ideas that each underlined word or phrase refers to.　　　ANALYZING

1. Paragraph D: At first, most of the scientists using <u>the new geologic term</u> were not geologists. _____

2. Sidebar: The boundaries between epochs are defined by changes preserved in sedimentary rocks—for example, the emergence of one type of commonly fossilized organism, or the disappearance of <u>another</u>. _____

3. Paragraph J: Probably the most significant change, from a geologic perspective, is <u>one</u> that's invisible to us—the change in the composition of the atmosphere. _____

4. Paragraph K: The most recent <u>one</u>—which is believed to have been caused by the impact of an asteroid—took place 65 million years ago, at the end of the Cretaceous period. _____

Deforestation threatens the habitats of many species of animals.

TREES OF LIFE

BEFORE VIEWING

DISCUSSION **A** How does deforestation affect our planet? Note your ideas below. Then discuss with a partner.

_____

_____

LEARNING ABOUT THE TOPIC **B** Read the information. Then answer the questions.

Rain forests provide habitats for thousands of species of animals. However, they also provide humans with many useful resources such as fruits and spices. Perhaps the most valuable rain forest resources, however, are medicinal plants. Scientists use rain forest plants to create drugs for many serious health problems. The bark of the cinchona tree, for example, is used to make quinine—a medication used to treat malaria. It is thought that scientists have analyzed less than one percent of rain forest plants, so there are probably hundreds, if not thousands, of medicinal plants that remain undiscovered.

1. What benefits of rain forests are mentioned in the paragraph above?

_____

2. How do you think deforestation would affect our ability to treat serious illnesses?

_____

C Read these extracts from the video. Match the correct form of each **bold** word to its definition.

VOCABULARY IN CONTEXT

> "At the current rate of **destruction**, the world's rain forests will completely disappear within a hundred years."
>
> "Forests are also destroyed as a result of growing urban sprawl, as land is developed for **dwellings**."
>
> "And while some plant and animal species are gone forever, **combatting** deforestation can help prevent further loss of biodiversity."

1. _____ (v) to fight against

2. _____ (n) a house or home

3. _____ (n) the act of damaging something completely

WHILE VIEWING

A ▶ Read the sentences below. Watch the video. Circle **T** for true or **F** for false.

UNDERSTANDING MAIN IDEAS

a. Transportation produces more greenhouse gases than forestry and agriculture. **T   F**

b. Over 80 percent of land animals live in forests. **T   F**

c. Increases in the size of urban areas is the primary cause of deforestation. **T   F**

B ▶ Watch the video again. Complete the notes below.

UNDERSTANDING CAUSES AND EFFECTS

DEFORESTATION	
Effects	**Causes**
1. Increases greenhouse gases in two ways: • [1]_____ releases CO_2 • Forests help to [2]_____ 2. Destroys [3]_____ Also effects people who use forests for [4]_____	1. [5]_____ is the main cause. 2. Logging for [6]_____ industries 3. Increasing [7]_____

AFTER VIEWING

A What are two signs of deforestation that future stratigraphers will notice? Look again at the reading passage for ideas. Note your answer below. Then discuss with a partner.

CRITICAL THINKING: SYNTHESIZING

_____

_____

Writing

EXPLORING WRITTEN ENGLISH

VOCABULARY FOR WRITING

A The following words and phrases can be useful when writing about the human impact on the planet. Find them in the reading passage. Use the context to guess their meanings. Then complete each definition.

preservation (paragraph G)	**relatively** (sidebar)	**subtle** (paragraph H)
tasked with (paragraph N)	**determine** (paragraph N)	**avert** (paragraph O)

1. To _____ something is to prevent it from happening.

2. If you _____ something, you figure it out.

3. If a person or group is _____ a duty, it is their responsibility to do it.

4. _____ refers to the protection of something over time.

5. If something is _____ big, it is big in comparison to something else.

6. If something is _____, it is not very noticeable.

NOTICING

B Read the sentences. Circle the words that the underlined words refer to.

1. Crutzen, who started the debate, thinks <u>its</u> real value won't lie in revisions to geology textbooks.
2. The process is likely to take years. As <u>it</u> drags on, the decision may well become easier.
3. Crutzen has suggested that the Anthropocene began in the late 18th century … Other scientists put the beginning of <u>the new epoch</u> in the middle of the 20th century …
4. As carbon dioxide warms the planet, <u>it</u> also seeps into the oceans and acidifies <u>them</u>.
5. To future geologists, Zalasiewicz says, our impact may look as sudden and profound as <u>that</u> of an asteroid.

Flower fields in California, United States

Writers use cohesive devices to emphasize key concepts they have already mentioned and to avoid repetition. Cohesive devices include reference words such as *it*, *these*, *those*, and *that*. They also include synonyms and word forms.

Reference Words and Synonyms:

In 2002, when Crutzen wrote up the Anthropocene idea in the journal *Nature*, **the concept** was immediately picked up by researchers working in a wide range of disciplines. Soon it began to appear regularly in the scientific press.

The writer uses *the concept* and *it* to refer to *the Anthropocene idea*.

Word Forms:

Way back in the 1870s, an Italian geologist named Antonio Stoppani proposed that people had introduced a new era, which he labeled the Anthropozoic. Stoppani's **proposal** was ignored; other scientists found it unscientific.

The writer uses *proposal* to refer to what Stoppani *proposed*.

C Use the cues to complete the second sentence in each pair below. Use reference words, synonyms, or word forms for the underlined words in the first sentence.

USING COHESIVE DEVICES

1. Cities are filled with structures made of glass, steel, and concrete. Many people might think that _____ are indestructible materials. (reference word)

2. Farming has had a huge impact on the world's landscapes. Around 38 percent of our planet's ice-free land is now used solely for _____. (synonym)

3. Humans have destroyed forests, built over animal habitats, and heated up the atmosphere with CO_2 emissions. Of all these _____, the changes in the atmosphere may leave the most lasting traces. (synonym)

4. By creating pedestrian-only streets in city centers, planners are reducing the amount of time people spend in cars. This _____ in car use will have a positive impact on the environment. (word form)

5. Chemicals used in pesticides may harm people and animals. These _____ compounds can have a negative impact on the soil and water as well. (word form)

WRITING SKILL Reviewing Essay Writing

An essay is a short piece of writing that includes an **introduction**, a **body**, and a **conclusion**. The introduction presents general information on the topic, and usually includes a **thesis statement**. The thesis statement presents the main idea of the entire essay. The body paragraphs support the thesis with facts, details, explanations, and other information. **Transitions** between paragraphs help the reader follow the essay. The conclusion restates the thesis and leaves the reader with a final thought on the topic.

You usually write an essay in response to an **essay prompt**. The prompt might be an instruction (*Describe/Explain . . .*), or it might be a question (*Why . . . ? To what extent . . . ? How . . . ?*). When you respond to a prompt, think about your position on the topic (which will become your thesis statement) and ways to support or explain your position (which may become the topic sentences of your body paragraphs).

CRITICAL THINKING: EVALUATING
D Read the following essay prompt. Circle the best thesis statement for it. Why is it the best? Discuss your answer with a partner.

What are some ways that people can help heal the planet through their food choices?

a. People can make much better food choices.

b. People can help heal the planet by making environmentally friendly food choices.

c. It's important that we start caring about the future of the planet right now.

CRITICAL THINKING: EVALUATING
E Think about ways to support or explain the thesis statement. Assume you are going to write three body paragraphs. Check (✓) the three best supporting ideas from the list below.

Make food choices that _____.

☐ a. are cheap   ☐ d. preserve endangered species

☐ b. promote health   ☐ e. use fewer resources such as water

☐ c. don't contribute to pollution

APPLYING
F Complete topic sentences for three body paragraphs based on the ideas you chose in exercise **E**.

One way that our food choices can help heal the planet is _____
_____

Another way is _____
_____

Finally, _____
_____

DISCUSSION
G Discuss the following essay prompt. Think of a good thesis statement and at least three possible ideas to support it. Share your ideas with a partner.

Describe new policies that would improve the quality of life at your college or school.

REVISING PRACTICE

The draft below is an essay about improving quality of life in cities. Follow the steps to create a better second draft.

1. Add the sentences (a–c) in the most suitable spaces.

   a. This reduces energy use as well as cost.
   b. By instituting these and other methods to make cities more livable and environmentally friendly, we can look forward to a happy and healthy future as our cities grow.
   c. Green spaces have a positive impact on a community.

2. Now fix the following problems (a–c) with the essay.

   a. Replace the **bold** word in paragraph B with a cohesive device.
   b. Replace the **bold** word in paragraph C with a cohesive device.
   c. Cross out one sentence that does not relate to the topic of the essay in paragraph D.

A

Cities are growing in size and in population. Will they have a harmful impact on the environment as they grow? Not necessarily. Many city planners have solutions to make cities and the people who live in them healthier and happier, while at the same time having a positive impact on the environment. Three ways to improve cities include creating green spaces, developing mixed-use areas, and encouraging building owners to transform their rooftops into gardens.

B

_____ **Green spaces** are protected areas that remain undeveloped, such as parks or other open areas. Increasing the number of them in a city has several advantages. Green spaces make a city more attractive, as plants and other features—such as streams and rocks—are left in their natural state. They also provide peaceful recreation areas for city dwellers. People can walk, hike, bicycle, and picnic in these areas away from the hustle and bustle of city life. Trees also shelter the area from the noise and traffic of the city while improving the air quality.

C

Another way to improve the quality of life in cities is the development of mixed-use areas. **Mixed-use** areas combine several purposes in one space. One of these areas, for example, may contain offices and businesses, apartments, and entertainment facilities. Ideally, mixed-use developments attract people who want to live and work in the same area. The benefits to the community are significant because these developments allow people to reduce the amount of time they spend in cars—driving to work and running errands—which in turn reduces air pollution. Creating mixed-use areas with pedestrian- and bicycle-only streets further lessens the impact on the environment, and it can also encourage better health and fitness as citizens spend less time in cars.

D

Finally, encouraging building owners to convert their rooftops into high-rise gardens and farms can bring about dramatic changes to city life and improve the environment at the same time. Rooftop gardens insulate buildings. For example, in areas that have hot summer weather, rooftop gardens can cool buildings so that they don't require as much air conditioning. _____ Gardens that are used to grow organic fruits and vegetables—as opposed to those grown with chemical compounds—can also improve the quality of life for city dwellers, especially if they live in areas where access to fresh produce is limited. Organic fruits and vegetables are increasingly available in many cities. Limiting the use of harmful pesticides through organic gardening is good for the planet and for human health, too.

E

Green spaces, mixed-use areas, and rooftop gardens are just a few of the ways that we can lessen the impact of cities on the planet. _____

EDITING PRACTICE

Read the information below. Then edit the sentences (1–3) to make them clearer.

When using cohesive devices, remember to:

- use pronouns that match the referent in gender and number.

- make sure a pronoun clearly refers to a specific word or idea. Sometimes it's better to repeat words or use synonyms for clarity.

- choose the correct synonym when using a dictionary or thesaurus.

1. One reason to limit the use of pesticides is that it contains harmful compounds.

2. Some people are installing rooftop gardens and using solar panels in their homes. It can save money and resources.

3. Many fish species have become extinct and, as a result, there is less biodiversity in our oceans. They are a problem, because they upset the natural balance of the oceans' ecosystems.

UNIT REVIEW

Answer the following questions.

1. What are three examples of the human impact on our planet?

   _____

   _____

2. Why are forests important to our planet?

   _____

   _____

3. What is an example of a cohesive device?

   _____

   _____

4. Do you remember the meanings of these words? Check (✓) the ones you know. Look back at the unit and review the ones you don't know.

   ☐ atmosphere   ☐ erosion **AWL**

   ☐ concept **AWL**   ☐ essentially

   ☐ consequence **AWL**   ☐ fertilizer

   ☐ criteria **AWL**   ☐ perspective **AWL**

   ☐ current   ☐ profound

   ☐ devoted to **AWL**   ☐ satisfy

   ☐ dramatic **AWL**   ☐ transform **AWL**

   ☐ eliminate **AWL**

NOTES

MEDICAL INNOVATIONS

4

A drone delivers medical supplies to a clinic in Virginia, U.S.A.

THINK AND DISCUSS

1 In what ways have medical treatments

A Look at the information on these pages and answer the questions.

1. Read the information in the timeline. Which of these medical firsts do you think was the most important? Why?
2. What is one other medical innovation that you can add to the timeline?

B Match the correct form of the words in blue to their definitions.

_____ (n) a way of doing something

_____ (v) to be able to do something that is challenging

_____ (n) a person who leads the way in a new area of knowledge

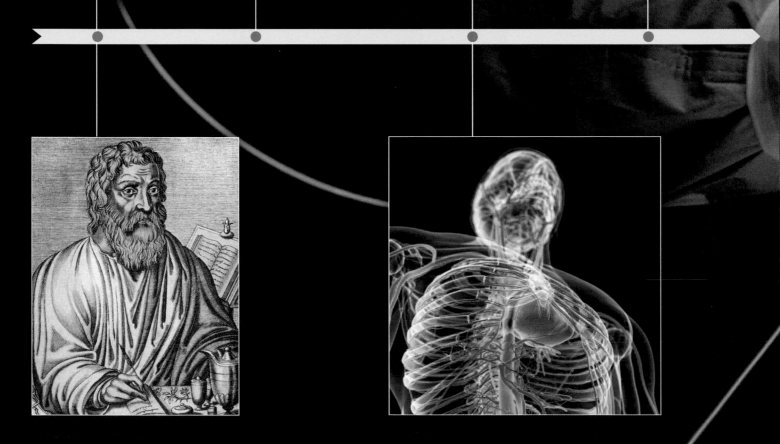

400 B.C.
First scientific study of medicine

The Greek physician Hippocrates first recognized that disease is caused by a patient's environment, diet, and/or daily habits. This discovery is regarded as the beginning of modern medicine.

4th Century A.D.
First hospitals

The earliest hospitals with trained doctors appeared in what is now Turkey. By the ninth century, hospitals were common in Islamic cities such as Baghdad and Cairo.

1628
First theory of blood circulation

English physician William Harvey proved that the beating heart drives the body's blood circulation.

1846
First use of anesthesia

American dentist William Morton developed a method for anesthetizing patients using a gas called ether. The patient fell asleep and felt no pain as Morton took out his rotten tooth.

MEDICAL FIRSTS

1859
First theory of germs and disease
French chemist Louis Pasteur was a pioneer in microbiology. He revealed how germs can infect people and make them sick.

1928
First use of penicillin
The Scottish biologist Alexander Fleming discovered the effect of penicillin on bacteria. Penicillin is still used today as an antibiotic to fight infection.

1983
First discovery of HIV virus
A team of French scientists managed to solve one of the biggest mysteries of modern disease when it discovered that the cause of AIDS was the human immunodeficiency virus (HIV).

2015
First bionic eye
A medical technology company—Second Sight—developed an implant that helps blind people see light.

Reading 1

PREPARING TO READ

A The words in **blue** below are used in Reading 1. Read the sentences. Then match the correct form of each word to its definition.

> It is important to improve **existing** hospitals as well as build new ones.
>
> Medical students study **general** topics before choosing a specific area to specialize in.
>
> The ancient Greek and Roman **civilizations** developed their own medical tools and techniques.
>
> People should stay home when they have the flu so that they don't **spread** it to other people.
>
> The *Merck* **Manual** *of Diagnosis and Therapy* is one of the oldest medical textbooks in English.
>
> Persian physician Ibn Sina **compiled** his medical knowledge in *The Canon of Medicine*, which includes basic **concepts** about the human body and the uses of medical substances.

1. _____ (adj) available at the time

2. _____ (n) an idea about something

3. _____ (adj) not relating to a particular area

4. _____ (v) to reach more people or a larger area

5. _____ (v) to gather information to create a book or a report

6. _____ (n) a group of people with its own culture and way of life

7. _____ (n) a book that includes instructions on how to do something

B Discuss these questions with a partner.

1. When you buy something new, such as a smartphone, do you prefer to read the **manual** or figure out how to use it on your own? Why?

2. How do you remember new **concepts** you learn in class? What **methods** do you use?

C How do you think medical knowledge has been passed down over the centuries? Discuss with a partner.

D Look at the photos and read the title of the reading passage. What do you think the passage is about? Check your idea as you read.

a. a medical innovator who lived in Spain many years ago

b. the man who built the first hospital in Europe

c. a doctor who found a cure for a common disease

THE HEALER OF CÓRDOBA

♪ Track 4

An illustration of Al-Zahrawi treating a patient

A   It is the year 1005. In the Andalusian[1] city of Medina Azahara, a woman is giving birth. Through the window of the delivery room, she can see the city's elaborate[2] columns, fountains, and finely polished marble terraces.[3] Her heart is pounding because she fears this is the last time she will see them. However, she has great faith in her doctor.

B   The doctor's name is Al-Zahrawi, and, in later years, he will be known as Abulcasis, one of the great **pioneers** of surgery. At the moment, all of Al-Zahrawi's attention is focused on the difficult birth. He sees that the baby must be turned before it can pass through the birth canal. From his medical bag, he takes out a tool that he made himself—a pair of forceps with a semicircular end designed to pull the fetus from the mother. In fact, he pioneered the use of forceps about 50 years earlier, when he was just starting his medical career.

[1] **Andalusia** is a region of southern Spain.
[2] If something is **elaborate**, it is richly decorated with a lot of detail.
[3] A **terrace** is a flat area of stone or grass next to a building.

MEDICAL INNOVATIONS   **77**

"Will my baby live?" the desperate mother **manages to** ask between contractions.[4] "Almost certainly," the doctor answers. "You have a healthy boy. But this next moment is going to be painful." The mother is happy to hear that her baby will live, but as the doctor warned, the pain is terrible. It is so strong that she loses consciousness for a few moments, but soon she is awakened by her baby's healthy cry.

THE METHOD OF MEDICINE

The forceps are just one of 200 surgical instruments that Al-Zahrawi described in his work *Al-Tasrif*, or *The Method of Medicine*. Many of the instruments and techniques described in its pages were invented by Al-Zahrawi himself. Born in Córdoba in 936, Al-Zahrawi was a doctor for the Spanish royal court at the height of Muslim **civilization** in Spain. During his long career, he **compiled** huge amounts of medical knowledge based on **existing** texts and his own experience.

Al-Zahrawi brought all his knowledge together in *Al-Tasrif*. This work was a 30-volume collection of all medical knowledge available at the time. The collection begins with basic **concepts**. Then it moves on from these **general** ideas to describe hundreds of topics including food and nutrition, skin diseases, and poisons. The final—and longest—volume deals with surgery. It includes treatments for head and spinal injuries, as well as techniques for amputating[5] a limb without killing the patient.

[4] **Contractions** are the tightening of the muscles of the uterus during childbirth.
[5] **Amputating** a person's arm or leg means cutting all or part of it off in an operation.

▼ **The ruins of Medina Azahara Palace, near Córdoba, Spain**

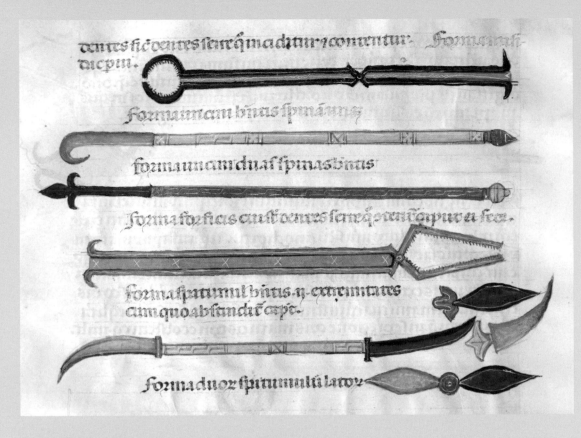

F The work also includes the world's first illustrations of surgical instruments, such as knives, scissors, and forceps. Many of the instruments look very familiar today. Al-Zahrawi's tools were helpful for treating conditions such as bone diseases, bladder[6] stones, and wounds. They were also useful in childbirth. One of Al-Zahrawi's most important inventions was the use of catgut[7] for sewing up a patient internally after surgery. Catgut is a strong substance that can dissolve[8] naturally in the body. It is still sometimes used in surgeries today.

G Al-Zahrawi wrote about his instruments and **methods** to share his knowledge with others, including doctors who came after him. However, he surely could not have predicted how his work would educate and inform surgeons centuries after his death. There was only a single handwritten copy of *Al-Tasrif*. It was almost lost during an attack on the area in 1010, when many buildings and documents were destroyed. Fortunately, the work was saved. Over the next several decades, it was passed from person to person. Eventually, *Al-Tasrif* was translated into Latin from its original Arabic. More than four centuries after they were written, parts of the work were finally printed in 1471.

H The printed translation **spread** Al-Zahrawi's knowledge throughout Europe. There, it had an enormous influence on medicine and surgery. *The Method of Medicine* was used as a **manual** for surgery in medical schools for centuries. Al-Zahrawi's legacy[9] can still be seen in many of the techniques and tools used in modern hospitals. He continues to be regarded as the "father of modern surgery."

[6] Your **bladder** is the part of your body where urine is stored.
[7] **Catgut** is a strong cord or thread made from the intestines of animals, usually sheep.
[8] To **dissolve** is to melt away or disappear.
[9] A person's **legacy** is something that they do or create that will continue to exist after they are dead.

UNDERSTANDING THE READING

SUMMARIZING **A** Complete the summary of the passage. Write no more than two words in each space.

Al-Zahrawi was a medical innovator who lived in ¹_____ during the 11th century. He worked as a doctor for the Spanish ²_____. Al-Zahrawi was a(n) ³_____ in the use of various surgical tools and techniques. He compiled all of his ⁴_____ in his work called *Al-Tasrif*. A translation of his writings—*The Method of Medicine*—was used to teach ⁵_____ in European medical schools for hundreds of years. Many of his inventions and methods are still in use today.

IDENTIFYING MAIN IDEAS **B** Match each section from the passage to its main idea.

_____ 1. Paragraphs A–C   a. Al-Zahrawi's writings were almost destroyed, but they were saved and then translated.

_____ 2. Paragraph D   b. Al-Zahrawi's writings contain detailed information about medical treatments and tools.

_____ 3. Paragraphs E–F   c. Al-Zahrawi's work helped doctors for centuries, and continues to influence medicine today.

_____ 4. Paragraph G   d. Al-Zahrawi helps a woman through a difficult birth using a medical tool he designed.

_____ 5. Paragraph H   e. Al-Zahrawi developed numerous medical techniques during his career.

> **CRITICAL THINKING**   Based on information the writer provides and their use of language, you can **infer**, or guess, the **writer's purpose**. What does the writer want to do: entertain, inform, or persuade? How does the writer use language to achieve their purpose?

CRITICAL THINKING: INFERRING PURPOSE **C** Answer the questions and discuss your answers with a partner.

1. How does the reading passage begin?
   a. with a factual description of Al-Zahrawi's later career
   b. with a story about how Al-Zahrawi helped a patient
   c. with an opinion about Al-Zahrawi's skills as a doctor

2. Skim the verbs in paragraphs A–C. What form are most of them in?
   a. past tense
   b. present tense
   c. future tense

3. Why do you think the writer started the passage this way?
   a. to describe an important moment in Al-Zahrawi's career
   b. to explain Al-Zahrawi's reasons for becoming a doctor
   c. to make readers interested in Al-Zahrawi

D Put the events about Al-Zahrawi's life and achievements (a–f) on the timeline.

SEQUENCING

a. Al-Zahrawi was born.
b. The translated version of *Al-Tasrif* was printed.
c. *Al-Tasrif* was passed on through different people.
d. The original copy of *Al-Tasrif* was nearly lost.
e. Medical schools in Europe began using *The Method of Medicine* as a textbook.
f. Al-Zahrawi wrote about his knowledge and inventions in a 30-volume collection.

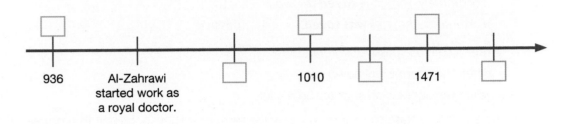

936   Al-Zahrawi started work as a royal doctor.   1010   1471

E Write short answers to these questions about Al-Zahrawi's work *Al-Tasrif*.

UNDERSTANDING DETAILS

1. What are two things described in the last volume of *Al-Tasrif*?

_____

2. What aspect of *Al-Tasrif* was unique at the time?

_____

3. Al-Zahrawi described the use of catgut in *Al-Tasrif*. How was this invention useful?

_____

4. How was *Al-Tasrif* nearly destroyed in 1010?

_____

5. How did *Al-Tasrif* become more widely known after Al-Zahrawi's death?

_____

F Write short answers to the questions below. Then discuss with a partner.

CRITICAL THINKING: REFLECTING

1. Imagine that *Al-Tasrif* had been destroyed in 1010. Would modern medicine be any different today? Why or why not?

_____

_____

2. Can you think of any other book or books that had a major impact on science or society? Why were they significant?

_____

_____

DEVELOPING READING SKILLS

READING SKILL Understanding Passive Sentences

Sentences can be active or passive. An active sentence focuses on the agent of an action (the subject is performing the action). A passive sentence, on the other hand, focuses on the recipient of an action (the subject is being "acted upon").

> Fortunately, <u>someone</u> **saved** the work. (active)
> Fortunately, <u>the work</u> **was saved**. (passive)

Writers often use passive sentences:

- when the agent is unknown.
- when the agent is obvious to the reader.

When writers state the agent in a passive sentence, they include it in a phrase starting with *by*.

> <u>Al-Tasrif</u> was written **by** <u>Al-Zahrawi</u>.

However, the main focus of the sentence is still on the recipient (*Al-Tasrif*) of the action and not the agent (Al-Zahrawi).

IDENTIFYING PASSIVE SENTENCES

A Read the sentences from the reading passage. Write P if the underlined verb is passive and A if it is active.

_____ 1. He sees that the baby must <u>be turned</u> before it can pass through the birth canal.

_____ 2. Al-Zahrawi <u>brought</u> all his knowledge together in *Al-Tasrif*.

_____ 3. It <u>is</u> still <u>used</u> in surgeries today.

_____ 4. In fact, he <u>pioneered</u> the use of forceps about 50 years earlier, when he was just starting his medical career.

UNDERSTANDING PASSIVE SENTENCES

B Read the sentences (a–c) below. Then match each description (1–4) to one or more of the sentences.

a. Eventually, *Al-Tasrif* was translated into Latin from its original Arabic.

b. Many of the instruments and techniques were invented by Al-Zahrawi himself.

c. *The Method of Medicine* was used as a manual for surgery in medical schools for centuries.

_____ 1. The sentence has an agent.

_____ 2. The sentence doesn't have an agent.

_____ 3. The agent is not mentioned because it is obvious.

_____ 4. The agent is not mentioned because it is unknown.

HEALTHCARE INNOVATOR

National Geographic
Explorer Aydogan
Ozcan uses cell phone
technology to test people
for infectious diseases.

BEFORE VIEWING

A Read the caption of the photo. How do you think a cell phone might be used for testing people's health? Discuss with a partner.

PREDICTING

B Read the information about infectious diseases. Note two reasons why they are a problem in developing areas. Then discuss with a partner.

LEARNING ABOUT THE TOPIC

Infectious diseases can be spread from one person to another. Two common infectious diseases are malaria and tuberculosis. In 2015, there were over two hundred million malaria cases worldwide—90 percent of which occurred in Africa. Tuberculosis is a lung infection caused by bacteria. In 2015, about ten million people suffered from the disease, and almost two million died from it. More than half of tuberculosis cases occurred in six countries, such as India, Indonesia, and Nigeria. Many infectious diseases like these are treatable. However, lack of access to proper medical care makes it difficult to cure these diseases globally.

_____

_____

C The words in **bold** below are used in the video. Read the sentences. Then match each word to its definition.

> Doctors can use X-rays to **diagnose** medical problems, but sometimes they can determine patients' illnesses with just a physical examination.
>
> After a patient takes a blood test, lab technicians **process** the blood sample.
>
> Doctors use various machines to **monitor** a patient's blood pressure and heart rate.

1. _____ (v) to regularly check the progress of something

2. _____ (v) to identify (an illness or a disease)

3. _____ (v) to take in and analyze for information

WHILE VIEWING

A ▶ Watch the video. Why is the cell phone a suitable device to use as a diagnostic tool? Check (✓) the reasons.

☐ 1. Many people in developing countries own cell phones.

☐ 2. The diagnosis is more accurate than traditional test kits.

☐ 3. It provides almost instant test results.

☐ 4. It allows regional health information to be collected and studied.

B ▶ Watch the video again. Complete the steps for using the cell phone as a diagnostic tool.

1. Insert the _____ onto the back of the phone.

2. Select _____ on the menu.

3. An image of the _____ appears on-screen.

4. The _____ taps on the image of the diagnostic test.

5. The app _____ the image and produces the result.

6. The _____ is sent to a central server for healthcare workers to use.

AFTER VIEWING

A How else might cell phones be used for monitoring health or providing healthcare services? List two ideas and discuss with a partner.

_____

_____

B How do you think Ozcan's data could be used? Who would it be useful for? Discuss with a partner.

Reading 2

PREPARING TO READ

BUILDING VOCABULARY

A The words and phrases in **blue** below are used in Reading 2. Read the paragraph. Then match the correct form of each word or phrase to its definition.

Major advances are **taking place** in the field of prosthetics—**artificial** limbs made for people who have lost their arms or legs. Scientists have moved beyond **replacement** limbs made of plastic and metal. Instead, they are **seeking** to create robotic limbs that are more lifelike. For example, they are working to make limbs that allow the wearer to have a sense of touch. These limbs are in the **experimental** stages now, but if this **inventive** idea becomes a reality, it will be a **breakthrough** in medical technology. Users will have replacement limbs that look, feel, and operate almost exactly like real limbs.

1. _____ (v) to look to find

2. _____ (v) to happen or occur

3. _____ (adj) creative, innovative

4. _____ (adj) still being tested

5. _____ (adj) made by humans and not by nature

6. _____ (n) a person or thing that takes the place of another

7. _____ (n) a sudden improvement in knowledge or technology

BUILDING VOCABULARY

B Read the sentences in the box. Then match each word in **blue** to its definition.

> Effective testing and early diagnosis have caused a **decline** in death rates of certain cancer types.
>
> **Survival** rates for cancer patients are much higher than they were 50 years ago; today, people with some types of cancer can live long lives.
>
> If you need blood and receive the wrong blood type, your body will **reject** it.

1. _____ (n) the continuation of life

2. _____ (n) a reduction in quality, amount, or number

3. _____ (v) to refuse to accept

USING VOCABULARY

C What recent medical **breakthroughs** do you know of? Discuss with a partner.

PREDICTING

D Look at the title, headings, and photos in the reading passage. What is the passage about? Check your idea as you read.

a. two recent advances in medical technology

b. the main challenges of medical transplants

c. the history of biotechnology

MEDICAL FRONTIERS

🎧 Track 5

A For centuries, medical pioneers have refined a variety of methods and medicines to treat sickness, injury, and disability, enabling people to live longer and healthier lives. Two of the most exciting **breakthroughs** in medical science today are regenerative medicine and nanotechnology.

GROWING BODY PARTS

B "A salamander[1] can grow back its leg. Why can't a human do the same?" asked Peruvian-born surgeon Dr. Anthony Atala. The question, a reference to work aiming to grow new limbs for wounded soldiers, captures the **inventive** spirit of regenerative medicine. This innovative field **seeks** to provide patients with **replacement** body parts. These parts are not made of steel; they are the real thing—living cells, tissue, and even organs.

C Regenerative medicine is still mostly **experimental** and limited to procedures such as growing sheets of skin on burn wounds. One of its most significant advances **took place** in 1999. A research group at North Carolina's Wake Forest Institute for Regenerative Medicine successfully replaced a bladder with one grown in a lab. Since then, the team—led by Dr. Atala—has created a variety of other tissues and organs, from kidneys to ears.

D The field of regenerative medicine is based on the first successful donor tissue and bone transplants done in the early 20th century. However, donor organs are not always the best option. First of all, they are in short supply. In the United States alone, more than 100,000 people are waiting for organ transplants—many people die while waiting for an available organ. Secondly, a patient's body may **reject** the donor organ. With regenerative medicine, however, tissues are grown from a patient's own cells and will not be rejected.

[1] A **salamander** is a small lizard-like animal that lives on land and in water.

E Today, several labs are working to create **artificial** body parts that are made from a patient's own cells. Scientists at Columbia University and Yale University have grown a jawbone and a lung. At the University of Minnesota, Dr. Doris Taylor has created a beating bioartificial rat heart. Dr. Atala's team has had long-term success with bioengineered bladders for young patients with spina bifida.[2] And at the University of Michigan, Dr. H. David Humes has created an artificial kidney.

F So far, the kidney procedure has only been used successfully with sheep. However, there is hope that one day it will be possible to implant a similar kidney in a human patient. The continuing research of scientists such as these may eventually make donor organs unnecessary. As a result, individuals may have significantly increased chances of **survival**.

[2] **Spina bifida** is a birth defect that involves the incomplete development of the spinal cord.

▽ **An artificial human nose created by Dr. Atala and his team**

How to (Re)grow a Kidney

More people are waiting for a kidney than any other organ, but it's one of the hardest to grow. Here is the strategy being followed by the research group at Wake Forest in its search to create the first transplantable bioartificial human kidney.

1
Sample a tiny bit of the patient's kidney.

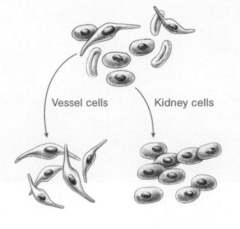

Vessel cells   Kidney cells

2
Sort kidney tissue cells from those of blood vessels running through it.

3
Multiply both types of cells in lab cultures.

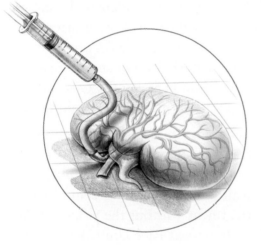

4
Inject the cultured cells of the patient into a scaffold,[3] which is made by washing a pig kidney with mild detergent[4] until the pig cells are gone and only the tough collagen remains.

5
Incubate[5] at 98.6°F (37°C) in a bioreactor that delivers oxygen and nutrients to the growing tissue.

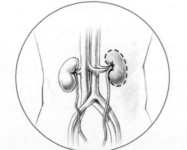

6
Implant a functioning human organ into the patient.

[3] A **scaffold** is a supporting structure.
[4] **Detergent** is a type of soap.
[5] To **incubate** something is to put it in an environment with a specific temperature for it to develop or grow.

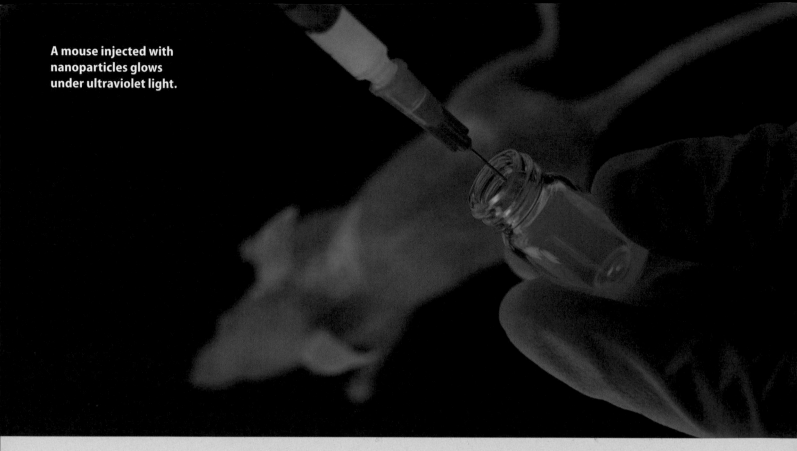

A mouse injected with nanoparticles glows under ultraviolet light.

USING NANOTECHNOLOGY

G The main thing to know about nanotechnology is that it is small—really small. *Nano-* is a prefix that means "dwarf"[6] in Greek. It is short for *nanometer*—one-billionth of a meter. To get an idea of how small a nanometer is, a comma (,) consists of about half a million nanometers. The nail on your little finger is about ten million nanometers across. To put it another way, a nanometer is the amount a man's beard grows in the time it takes him to lift a razor to his face.

H How can nanotechnology be applied to medicine? One of the potential applications is as an aid in surgery. Scientists at Rice University have used a solution of tiny silica[7] balls covered with gold to reconnect two pieces of animal tissue. These balls are called nanoshells. Someday soon, surgeons may be able to use a nanoshell treatment like this to reconnect blood vessels that have been cut during surgery. "One of the hardest things a doctor has to do during a kidney or heart transplant is reattach cut arteries," says André Gobin, a graduate student at Rice. "They have to sew the ends [of cut arteries] together with tiny stitches. Leaks are a big problem." The nanoshells will enable a surgeon to make a clean join between the two ends of a cut artery, preventing blood from leaking out.

I Nanotechnology may also help cancer patients. Traditional cancer treatments are severe and may cause a decline in the patient's health. However, nanotechnology promises treatment without the risks or side effects. Researchers at Rice University have engineered nanoshells that are about 120 nanometers wide—about 170 times smaller than a cancer cell. When they are injected into the bloodstream, they can enter tumors.[8] When an infrared laser is focused on the tumor, the light passes through healthy tissue but heats up the nanoshells. In laboratory tests using mice, the treatment killed cancer cells while leaving healthy tissue unharmed. The technique has the potential one day to be applied to human cancer patients.

[6] The word **dwarf** is used to describe something small.

[7] **Silica** is a material used for making glass and ceramics. It often exists in sand.

[8] A **tumor** is a mass of diseased or abnormal cells that has grown inside a person's or an animal's body.

UNDERSTANDING THE READING

A Complete the summary of the passage. Write no more than two words in each space.

Growing Body Parts

The field of regenerative medicine involves using a patient's [1]_____

to grow replacement body parts. This is possibly a more effective way to treat patients who

require [2]_____. Although the procedure is still mostly

[3]_____, scientists hope to successfully grow organs such as kidneys

for [4]_____ patients in the future.

Using Nanotechnology

Nanotechnology in medicine involves using very small particles to treat patients. For

example, some scientists have created tiny balls covered in gold called

[5]_____. These could help prevent blood from

[6]_____ when doctors are sewing up a patient during surgery. They

could also help [7]_____ patients by reducing the risks and

[8]_____ of treatment.

B According to the passage, what are some benefits of regenerative medicine? Check (✓) the ones mentioned.

☐ 1. shorter waiting time for an available organ

☐ 2. longer lasting than a donor organ

☐ 3. higher chance of patient's body accepting the new organ

☐ 4. cheaper than organ transplant surgeries

C Match each innovation in regenerative medicine to a scientist or group of scientists (a–e). Then complete the notes about the innovations using information from the passage.

a. Dr. Atala and team
b. Dr. Doris Taylor
c. Dr. H. David Humes
d. Researchers at Rice University
e. Scientists at Columbia University and Yale University

Scientist(s)	Innovation
	Bioengineered jawbone and lung
	Bioartificial rat heart
	Bioengineered bladder • _____ success with young patients with spinal problems
	Artificial kidney • Has been successfully used in _____ • May be possible to _____ a kidney in humans one day
	Nanoshell treatment • Could be used to reconnect _____ during surgery • Could be used to kill cancer cells without harming _____

D Put the steps for growing a kidney in order (1–6).

_____ a. Place the kidney into the patient.

_____ b. Take some cells from the patient's kidney.

_____ c. Allow the cells to increase in number in a culture.

_____ d. Separate the kidney cells from blood vessel cells.

_____ e. Keep the growing kidney tissue at body temperature.

_____ f. Place the cells in an animal kidney that has been cleaned and treated.

E Find and underline the following words and phrases in **bold** in the reading passage. Use context to identify their meanings. Then complete the definitions with your own words.

1. Paragraph A: If someone has **refined** something, they have _____ it by making small changes.

2. Paragraph D: If something is **in short supply**, there _____ of it available.

3. Paragraph G: "To **put it another way**" means to _____.

4. Paragraph H: If you **reattach** two things, you _____.

F Read the sentences from the reading passage. For each item, circle the noun that the **bold** pronoun refers to.

1. These parts are not made of steel; **they** are the real thing—living cells, tissue, and even organs.

2. However, donor organs are not always the best option. First of all, **they** are in short supply.

3. "One of the hardest things doctors have to do during a kidney or heart transplant is reattach cut arteries," says André Gobin, a graduate student at Rice. "**They** have to sew the ends [of cut arteries] together with tiny stitches."

4. Researchers at Rice University have engineered nanoshells that are about 120 nanometers wide—about 170 times smaller than a cancer cell. When **they** are injected into the bloodstream, they can enter tumors.

G How is Al-Zahrawi's use of catgut and Rice University's use of nanoshells similar? Write an answer and then discuss your idea with a partner.

Both catgut and nanoshells can be used _____

_____

UNIT REVIEW

Answer the following questions.

1. What is one ancient medical innovation and one modern one?

   _____

   _____

   _____

2. When reading, why is it important to infer the writer's purpose?

   _____

   _____

   _____

3. Do you remember the meanings of these words? Check (✔) the ones you know. Look back at the unit and review the ones you don't know.

Reading 1:

☐ civilization ☐ compile `AWL` ☐ concept `AWL`

☐ existing ☐ general ☐ manage to

☐ manual `AWL` ☐ method `AWL` ☐ pioneer

☐ spread

Reading 2:

☐ artificial ☐ breakthrough ☐ decline `AWL`

☐ experimental ☐ inventive ☐ reject `AWL`

☐ replacement ☐ seek ☐ survival

☐ take place

VOCABULARY EXTENSION   UNIT 1

Adjectives and Nouns Ending In -ive

Most words ending in -ive are adjectives, though some can also be used as nouns. For instance, *alternative* can be used as an adjective (*There is an alternative plan.*) or a noun (*The alternative won't work.*).

Read the sentences below. Label each underlined word as N if it is a noun or A if it is an adjective.

1. The <u>distinctive</u> design of the Eiffel Tower makes it a well-known icon worldwide.

2. One of the <u>objectives</u> of sustainable tourism is to manage tourist destinations in a way that preserves their original state.

3. The Mayan are <u>native</u> people who live in modern-day Mexico, Honduras, and Guatemala.

4. Many companies hire sales <u>representatives</u> to sell their products to customers.

5. Companies with a strong online presence have a <u>relative</u> advantage over those companies that do not.

6. Solar power is one example of an <u>alternative</u> energy source.

VOCABULARY EXTENSION   UNIT 3

WORD FORMS Adjectives Ending in -ic

For adjectives, the suffix -ic means "having the characteristics of." For example, *dramatic* means that something has the characteristics of a drama. To change an -ic adjective into an adverb, add -ally.

A Complete the chart. Use a dictionary to check your spelling.

Noun	Adjective	Adverb
academy		
	artistic	
athlete		
		atmospherically
	dramatic	
energy		
		linguistically

Collocations are words that often go together. Here are some common collocations with the adjective *dramatic*.

dramatic **change**	dramatic **decline**
dramatic **increase**	dramatic **improvement**
dramatic **effect**	dramatic **action**
dramatic **moment**	dramatic **difference**

B Circle the best option to complete each sentence.

1. The world's governments need to take dramatic **action** / **change** to halt climate change.

2. The most dramatic **difference** / **moment** came towards the end of the movie.

3. Unfortunately, the past year has seen a dramatic **decline** / **increase** in our company's profits.

4. Studying philosophy had a dramatic **change** / **effect** on the way I thought about life.

5. There is a dramatic **difference** / **improvement** between the lives of the richest and poorest people on Earth.

VOCABULARY EXTENSION   UNIT 4

WORD PARTNERS Antonyms

Antonyms are words that are opposite in meaning. For instance, the words *narrow* and *wide* are antonyms.

Match each word to its antonym. Use a dictionary to help you.

a. natural   b. specific   c. minimum   d. rise   e. accept

_____ 1. reject   _____ 2. decline   _____ 3. general   _____ 4. artificial   _____ 5. maximum

WRITING REFERENCE

UNIT 4
Reading Skill: Understanding Passive Sentences

An active sentence focuses on the subject (or the agent) of an action where the subject performs that action.

> *The city government built the hospital last year.*
> (The focus is on the subject *the city government*.)

A passive sentence focuses on the object (or the recipient) of an action. Use passive sentences when the agent is unknown or when the agent is unimportant in the context.

> *The hospital was built last year.*
> (The focus is on the object *the hospital*. It is not important to know who built it.)

Add *by* + the agent to passive sentences to show who did the action.

> *A bionic eye was developed by Second Sight.*

Passive sentences always include a form of *be* + the past participle form of the verb.

	Active	Passive
Simple Present	People still **use** Al-Zahrawi's instruments today.	Al-Zahrawi's instruments **are** still **used** today.
Simple Past	Luckily, no one **destroyed** his books.	Luckily, his books **weren't destroyed**.
Present Continuous	Surgeons **are studying** Al-Zahrawi's books today.	Al-Zahrawi's books **are being studied** today.

Brief Writer's Handbook

Understanding the Writing Process: The Seven Steps

The Assignment

Imagine that you have been given the following assignment: *Write an essay in which you discuss one aspect of vegetarianism.* What should you do first? What should you do second, third, and so on? There are many ways to write, but most good writers follow certain steps in the writing process. These steps are guidelines that are not always followed in order.

Look at this list of steps. Which ones do you regularly do? Which ones have you never done?

STEP 1: Choose a topic.

STEP 2: Brainstorm.

STEP 3: Outline.

STEP 4: Write the first draft.

STEP 5: Get feedback from a peer.

STEP 6: Revise the first draft.

STEP 7: Proofread the final draft.

Next, you will see how one student, Hamda, went through the steps to do the assignment. First, read the final essay that Hamda gave her teacher.

Essay 1

Better Living as a Vegetarian

1   The hamburger has become a worldwide cultural icon. Eating meat, especially beef, is an integral part of many diverse cultures. Studies show, however, that the consumption of large quantities of meat is a major contributing factor toward a great many deaths, including the unnecessarily high number of deaths from heart-related problems. Although it has caught on slowly in Western society, vegetarianism is a way of life that can help improve not only the quality of people's lives but also their longevity.

2   Surprising as it may sound, vegetarianism can have beneficial effects on the environment. Because demand for meat animals is so high, cattle are being raised in areas where rain forests once stood. As rain forest land is cleared in order to make room for cattle ranches, the environmental balance is upset; this imbalance could have serious consequences for humans. The article "Deforestation: The hidden cause of global warming" by Daniel Howden explains that much of the current global warming is due to depletion of the rain forests.

3   More important at an individual level is the question of how eating meat affects a person's health. Meat, unlike vegetables, can contain very large amounts of fat. Eating this fat has been connected—in some research cases—to certain kinds of cancer. In fact, *The St. Petersburg*

Times reports, "There was a statistically significant risk for . . . gastric cancer associated with consumption of all meat, red meat and processed meat" (Rao, 2006). If people cut down on the amounts of meat they ate, they would automatically be lowering their risks of disease. Furthermore, eating animal fat can lead to obesity, and obesity can cause numerous health problems. For example, obesity can cause people to slow down and their heart to have to work harder. This results in high blood pressure. Meat is also high in cholesterol, and this only adds to health problems. With so much fat consumption worldwide, it is no wonder that heart disease is a leading killer.

4   If people followed vegetarian diets, they would not only be healthier but also live longer. Eating certain kinds of vegetables, such as broccoli, brussels sprouts, and cauliflower, has been shown to reduce the chance of contracting colon cancer later in life. Vegetables do not contain the "bad" fats that meat does. Vegetables do not contain cholesterol, either. Furthermore, native inhabitants of areas of the world where people eat more vegetables than meat, notably certain areas of Central Asia, routinely live to be over one hundred.

5   Some people argue that, human nature being what it is, it is unhealthy for humans to not eat meat. These same individuals say that humans are naturally carnivores and cannot help wanting to consume a juicy piece of red meat. However, anthropologists have shown that early humans ate meat only when other foods were not abundant. Man is inherently a herbivore, not a carnivore.

6   Numerous scientific studies have shown the benefits of vegetarianism for people in general. There is a common thread for those people who switch from eating meat to consuming only vegetable products. Although the change of diet is difficult at first, most never regret their decision to become a vegetarian. They feel better, and those around them comment that they look better than ever before. As more and more people are becoming aware of the risks associated with meat consumption, they too will make the change.

Steps in the Writing Process

Step 1: Choose a Topic

For this assignment, the topic was given: Write an essay on vegetarianism. As you consider the assignment topic, you have to think about what kind of essay you may want to write. Will you list different types of vegetarian diets? Will you talk about the history of vegetarianism? Will you argue that vegetarianism is or is not better than eating animal products?

Hamda chose to write an argumentative essay about vegetarianism to try to convince readers of its benefits. The instructor had explained that this essay was to be serious in nature and have facts to back up the claims made.

Step 2: Brainstorm

The next step for Hamda was to brainstorm.

In this step, you write every idea about your topic that pops into your head. Some of these ideas will be good, and some will be bad; write them all. The main purpose of brainstorming is to write as many ideas as you can think of. If one idea looks especially good, you might circle that idea or put a check next to it. If you write an idea and you know right away that you are not going to use it, you can cross it out.

Brainstorming methods include making lists, clustering similar ideas, or diagramming your thoughts.

Look at Hamda's brainstorming diagram on the topic of vegetarianism.

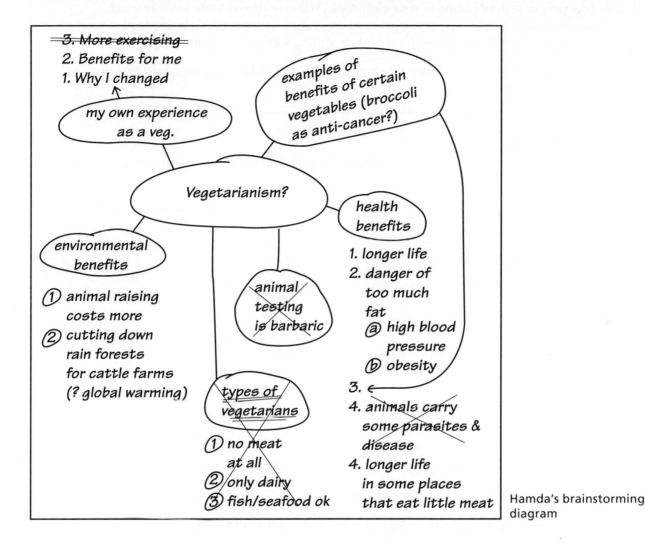

Hamda's brainstorming diagram

As you can see from the brainstorming diagram, Hamda considered many aspects of vegetarianism. Notice a few items in the diagram. As she organized her brainstorming, Hamda wrote "examples of benefits of certain vegetables" as a spoke on the wheel. Then she realized that this point would be a good number three in the list of health benefits, so she drew an arrow to show that she should move it there. Since one of Hamda's brainstorming ideas (types of vegetarians) seemed to lack supporting details and was not related to her other notes, she crossed it out.

Getting the Information

How would you get the information for this brainstorming exercise?

- You might read a book or an article about vegetarianism.

- You could spend time searching online for articles on the subject.

- You could write a short questionnaire to give to classmates asking them about their personal knowledge of vegetarian practices.

- You could also interview an expert on the topic, such as a nutritionist.

Step 3: Outline

Next, create an outline for the essay. Here is Hamda's rough outline that she wrote from her brainstorming notes.

I. Introduction

    A. Define vegetarianism

    B. List different types

    C. Thesis statement

II. Environmental benefits (Find sources to support!)

    A. Rain forests

    B. Global warming

III. Health issues (Find sources to support!)

    A. Too much fat from meat → obesity → diseases → cancer

    B. High blood pressure and heart disease

    C. Cancer-fighting properties of broccoli and cauliflower, etc.

IV. Counterargument and refutation

    A. Counterargument: Man is carnivore.

    B. Refutation

V. Conclusion

    A. Restate thesis

    B. Opinion: Life will improve.

Supporting Details

After you have chosen the main points for your essay you will need to develop some supporting details. You should include examples, reasons, explanations, definitions, or personal experiences. In some cases, such as this argumentative essay on vegetarianism, it is a good idea to include outside sources or expert opinions that back up your claims.

One common technique for generating supporting details is to ask specific questions about the topic, for example:

SUPPORT

What is it?

What happened?

How did this happen?

What is it like or not like? Why?

Step 4: Write the First Draft

Next, Hamda wrote her first draft. As she wrote each paragraph of the essay, she paid careful attention to the language she used. She chose a formal sentence structure including a variety of sentence types. In addition, her sentences varied in length, with the average sentence containing almost 20 words. (Sentences in conversation tend to be very short; sentences in academic writing tend to be longer.) Hamda also took great care in choosing appropriate vocabulary. In addition to specific terminology, such as *obesity, blood pressure,* and *consumption*, she avoided the conversational *you* in the essay, instead referring to *people* and *individuals*.

In this step, you use information from your brainstorming session and outline to write the essay. This first draft may contain many errors, such as misspellings, incomplete ideas, and comma errors. At this point, you should not worry about correcting the errors. The main thing is to put your ideas into sentences.

You may feel that you do not know what you think about the topic yet. In this case, it may be difficult for you to write, but it is important to just write, no matter what comes out. Sometimes writing helps you think, and as soon as you form a new thought, you can write it.

Better Living as a Vegetarian

Wow — too abrupt? You don't talk about hamburgers anymore??

(Do you like hamburgers?) Eating meat, especially beef, is an interesting part of the *vocabulary?*

daily life around the world. In addition, this high eating of meat is a major contributing *word choice?*

factor ~~thing~~ *causes* that makes a great many deaths, including the unnecessarily high number of

deaths from heart-related problems. Vegetarianism has caught on slowly in some parts

, and it of the world. (Vegetarianism) is a way of life that can help improve not only the quality of

people's lives but also people's longevity. → *the quality but also the length of people's lives*

This is not a topic sentence Because demand for meat animals is (so high., Cattle) are being raised in areas where

the rainforest once stood. As rain forest land is cleared in massive amounts in order to

make room for the cattle ranches, the environmental balance is being upset. This could

For example, *transition?* have serious consequences for us in both the near and long term. How much of the current

global warming is due to man's disturbing the rain forest?

You need a more specific topic relating to health.

(Meat contains a high amount of fat.) Eating this fat has been connected in research

cases with certain kinds of cancer. Furthermore, eating animal fat can lead to obesity, and

obesity can cause many different kinds of diseases, for example, obesity can cause people

to slow down and their heart to have to word harder. This results in high blood pressure.

Meat is high in cholesterol, and this only adds to the health problems. With the high

consumption of animal fat by so many people, it is no wonder that heart disease is a

leading killer.

Hamda's first draft

On the other hand, eating a vegetarian diet can improve a person's health. And

necessary?

vegetables taste so good. In fact, it can even save someone's life. Eating certain kinds

of vegetables, such as broccoli, brussels sprouts, and cauliflower, has been shown to

reduce the chance of having colon cancer later in life. *combine sentences?* Vegetables do not contain

the "bad" fats that meat does. Vegetables do not contain cholesterol, either. Native

inhabitants of areas of the world where mostly vegetables are consumed, notably

certain areas of the former Soviet republics, routinely live to be over one hundred.

Good sentence Although numerous scientific studies have shown the benefits of vegetarianism for people

in general, I know firsthand how my life has improved since I decided to give up meat entirely.

In 2006, I saw a TV program that discussed problems connected to animals that are raised for

food. The program showed how millions of chickens are raised in dirty, crowded conditions *not related to your topic*

until they are killed. The program also talked about how diseases can be spread from cow or

pig to humans due to unsanitary conditions. Shortly after I saw this show, I decided to try life

without eating meat. Although it was difficult at first, I have never regretted my decision to

become a vegetarian. I feel better and my friends tell me that I look better than ever before.

Being a vegetarian has many benefits. Try it.

This is too short!
How about making a prediction or suggestion for the reader? The previous paragraph told how the writer became a vegetarian, so doesn't it make sense for the conclusion to say something like "I'm sure your life will be better too if you become a vegetarian"?

I like this essay. You really need to work on the conclusion.

Making Changes

As you write the first draft, you may want to add information or take some out. In some cases, your first draft may not follow your outline exactly. That is OK. Writers do not always stick with their original plan or follow the steps in the writing process in order. Sometimes they go back and forth between steps. The writing process is much more like a cycle than a line.

Reread Hamda's first draft with her teacher's comments.

First Draft Tips

Here are some things to remember about the first draft copy:

- The first draft is not the final copy. Even native speakers who are good writers do not write an essay only one time. They rewrite as many times as necessary until the essay is the best that it can be.

- It is OK for you to make notes on your drafts; you can circle words, draw connecting lines, cross out words, or write new information. Make notes to yourself about what to change, what to add, or what to reconsider.

- If you cannot think of a word or an idea as you write, leave a blank space or circle. Then go back and fill in the space later. If you write a word that you know is not the right one, circle or underline it so you can fill in the right word later. Do not stop writing. When people read your draft, they can see these areas you are having trouble with and offer comments that may help.

- Do not be afraid to throw some sentences away if they do not sound right. Just as a good housekeeper throws away unnecessary things from the house, a good writer throws out unnecessary or wrong words or sentences.

The handwriting in the first draft is usually not neat. Sometimes it is so messy that only the writer can read it! Use a word-processing program, if possible, to make writing and revising easier.

Step 5: Get Feedback from a Peer

Hamda used Peer Editing Sheet 8 to get feedback on her essay draft. Peer editing is important in the writing process. You do not always see your own mistakes or places where information is missing because you are too close to the essay that you created. Ask someone to read your draft and give you feedback about your writing. Choose someone that you trust and feel comfortable with. While some people feel uneasy about peer editing, the result is almost always a better essay. Remember to be polite when you edit another student's paper.

Step 6: Revise the First Draft

This step consists of three parts:

1. React to the comments on the peer editing sheet.
2. Reread the essay and make changes.
3. Rewrite the essay one more time.

Step 7: Proofread the Final Draft

Most of the hard work is over now. In this step, the writer pretends to be a brand-new reader who has never seen the essay before. Proofread your essay for grammar, punctuation, and spelling errors and to see if the sentences flow smoothly.

Read Hamda's final paper again on pages 96–97.

Of course, the very last step is to turn the paper in to your teacher and hope that you get a good grade!

Writer's Note

Proofreading

One good way to proofread your essay is to set it aside for several hours or a day or two. The next time you read your essay, your head will be clearer and you will be more likely to see any problems. In fact, you will read the composition as another person would.

Editing Your Writing

While you must be comfortable writing quickly, you also need to be comfortable with improving your work. Writing an assignment is never a one-step process. For even the most gifted writers, it is often a multiple-step process. When you were completing your assignments in this book, you probably made some changes to your work to make it better. However, you may not have fixed all of the errors. The paper that you turned in to your teacher is called a first draft, which is sometimes referred to as a rough draft.

A first draft can often be improved. One way to improve an essay is to ask a classmate, friend, or teacher to read it and make suggestions. Your reader may discover that one of your paragraphs is missing a topic sentence, that you have made grammar mistakes, or that your essay needs better vocabulary choices. You may not always like or agree with the comments from a reader, but being open to changes will make you a better writer.

This section will help you become more familiar with how to identify and correct errors in your writing.

Step 1

Below is a student's first draft for a timed writing. The writing prompt for this assignment was "For most people, quitting a job is a very difficult decision. Why do people quit their jobs?" As you read the first draft, look for areas that need improvement and write your comments. For example, does the writer use the correct verb tenses? Is the punctuation correct? Is the vocabulary suitable for the intended audience? Does the essay have an appropriate hook?

There Are Many Reasons Why People Quit Their Jobs

Joann quit her high-paying job last week. She had had enough of her coworkers' abuse. Every day they would make fun of her and talk about her behind her back. Joann's work environment was too stressful, so she quit. Many employees quit their jobs. In fact, there are numerous reasons for this phenomenon.

First, the job does not fit the worker. Job seekers may accept a job without considering their skills. Is especially true when the economy is slowing and jobs are hard to find. The workers may try their best to change themselves depending on the work. However, at some point they realize that they are not cut out in this line of work and end up quitting. This lack of understanding or ability make people feel uncomfortable in their jobs. So they begin to look for other work.

Another reason people quit their jobs is the money. Why do people work in the first place? They work in order to make money. If employees are underpaid, he cannot earn enough to support himself or his family. The notion of working, earning a decent salary, and enjoy life is no longer possible. In this case, low-paid workers have no choice but to quit their jobs and search for a better-paying position.

Perhaps the biggest situation that leads people to quit their jobs is personality conflicts. It is really difficult for an employee to wake up every morning, knowing that they will be spending the next eight or nine hours in a dysfunctional environment. The problem can be with bosses or coworkers but the result is the same. Imagine working for a discriminate boss or colleagues which spread rumors. The stress levels increases until that employee cannot stand the idea of going to work. The employee quits his or her job in the hope of finding a more calm atmosphere somewhere else.

Work should not be a form of punishment. For those people who have problems with not feeling comfortable on the job, not getting paid enough, and not respected, it *does* feel like punishment. As a result, they quit and continue their search for a job that will give them a sense of pride, safety, and friends.

Step 2

Read the teacher's comments on the first draft of "There Are Many Reasons Why People Quit Their Jobs." Are these the same things that you noticed?

The title should NOT be a complete sentence.

There Are Many Reasons Why People Quit Their Jobs

Consider changing your hook/introduction. The introduction here is already explaining one of the reasons for quitting a job. This information should be in the body of the essay. Suggestion: Use a "historical" hook describing how people were more connected to their jobs in the past than they are now.

Joann quit her high-paying job last week. She had had enough of her coworkers' abuse. Every day they would make fun of her and talk about her behind her back. Joann's work environment was too stressful, so she quit. Many employees quit their jobs. In fact, there are numerous reasons for this phenomenon.

Try to use another transition phrase instead of first, second, etc.

add transition

(First,) the job does not fit the worker. ∧Job seekers may accept a job without considering their

word choice—be more specific   *fragment*

(skills.) <u>Is especially true when the economy is slowing and jobs are hard to find.</u> The workers may

word choice—better: "adapt to"

try their best to (change themselves depending on) the work. However, at some point they realize

prep

that they are not cut out (in) this line of work and end up quitting. This lack of understanding or

S-V agreement   *fragment*

ability (make) people feel uncomfortable in their (jobs. So) they begin to look for other work.

word choice—be more specific

Another reason people quit their jobs is the (money.) Why do people work in the first place?

They work in order to make money. If (employees) are underpaid, (he) cannot earn enough to

pronoun agreement

// not parallel—use "-ing"

support (himself) or (his family.) The notion of working, earning a decent salary, and (enjoy) life is

word choice   *Do you mean "underpaid"?*

no longer (possible.) In this case, (low-paid) workers have no choice but to quit their jobs and

search for a better-paying position.

word choice—too vague
Perhaps the (biggest) situation that leads people to quit their jobs is personality conflicts. It is

word choice—avoid using "really"   pronoun agreement

(really) difficult for an employee to wake up every morning, knowing that (they) will be spending

add another descriptive word here   word choice—too vague
the next eight or nine hours in a dysfunctional ˄ environment. The (problem) can be with bosses

punc. (add comma)   word choice
or coworkers but the result is the same. Imagine working for a (discriminate) boss or colleagues

word form   S-V agreement   write it out—better: "can no longer"
(which) spread rumors. The stress levels (increases) until that employee (can't) stand the idea of

add transition   word choice—better: "serene"
going to work. ˄ The employee quits his or her job in the hope of finding a more (calm) atmosphere

somewhere else.

thought of as   word choice
Work should not be ˄ a form of punishment. For those people who (have problems) with not

// not parallel—use "-ing"
feeling comfortable on the job, not getting paid enough, and (not respected,) it *does* feel like

punishment. As a result, they quit and continue their search for a job that will give them a

word choice—better: "camaraderie"
sense of pride, safety, and (friends.)

Step 3

Now read the second draft of this essay. How is it the same as the first draft? How is it different? Did the writer fix all the sentence mistakes?

Two Weeks' Notice

A generation ago, it was common for workers to stay at their place of employment for years and years. When it was time for these employees to retire, companies would offer a generous pension package and, sometimes, a token of appreciation, such as a watch, keychain, or other trinket. Oh, how times have changed. Nowadays, people—especially younger workers—jump from job to job like bees fly from flower to flower to pollinate. Some observers might say that today's workforce is not as serious as yesterday's. This is too simple an explanation, however. In today's society, fueled by globalization, recession, and other challenges, people quit their jobs for a number of valid reasons.

One reason for quitting a job is that the job does not fit the worker. In other words, job seekers may accept a job without considering their aptitude for it. This is especially true when the economy is slowing and jobs are hard to find. The workers may try their best to adapt themselves to the work. However, at some point they realize that they are not cut out for this line of work and end up quitting. This lack of understanding or ability makes people feel uncomfortable in their jobs, so they begin to look for other work.

Another reason people quit their jobs is the salary. Why do people work in the first place? They work in order to make money. If employees are underpaid, they cannot earn enough to support themselves or their families. The notion of working, earning a decent salary, and enjoying life is no longer viable. In this case, underpaid workers have no choice but to quit their jobs and search for a better-paying position.

Perhaps the most discouraging situation that leads people to quit their jobs is personality conflicts. It is extremely difficult for an employee to wake up every morning knowing that he or she will be spending the next eight or nine hours in a dysfunctional and often destructive environment. The discord can be with bosses or coworkers, but the result is the same. Imagine working for a bigoted boss or colleagues who spread rumors. The stress levels increase until that employee can no longer stand the idea of going to work. In the end, the employee quits his or her job with the hope of finding a more serene atmosphere somewhere else.

Work should not be thought of as a form of punishment. For those people who struggle with not feeling comfortable on the job, not getting paid enough, and not being respected, it *does* feel like punishment. As a result, they quit and continue their search for a job that will give them a sense of pride, safety, and camaraderie.

Sentence Types

English sentence structure includes three basic types of sentences: simple, compound, and complex. These labels indicate how the information in a sentence is organized, not how difficult the content is.

Simple Sentences

1. Simple sentences usually contain one subject and one verb.

    > S   V
    > [Kids] love television.

    > V   S   V
    > Does [this] sound like a normal routine?

2. Sometimes simple sentences can contain more than one subject or verb.

    > S   V
    > [Brazil and the United States] are large countries.

    > S   V   V
    > [Brazil] lies in South America and has a large population.

    > S   V   V
    > [We] traveled throughout Brazil and ended our trip in Argentina.

Compound Sentences

Compound sentences are usually made up of two simple sentences (independent clauses). Compound sentences need a coordinating conjunction (connector) to combine the two sentences. The coordinating conjunctions include:

> for   and   nor   but   or   yet   so

Many writers remember these conjunctions with the acronym *FANBOYS*. Each letter represents one conjunction: *F = for, A = and, N = nor, B = but, O = or, Y = yet,* and *S = so.*

Remember that a comma is always used before a coordinating conjunction that separates the two independent clauses.

> **for**   [Meagan] studied hard, **for** [she] wanted to pass the test.

> **and**   [Meagan] studied hard, **and** [her classmates] studied, too.

> **nor**   [Meagan] did not study hard, **nor** did [she] pass the test.

> **but**   [Meagan] studied hard, **but** [her brother] did not study at all.

> **or**   [Meagan] studied hard, **or** [she] would have failed the test.

> **yet**   [Meagan] studied hard, **yet** [she] was not happy with her grade.

> **so**   [Meagan] studied hard, **so** [the test] was easy for her.

Study the following examples of compound sentences. Draw a |box| around each subject, underline each verb, and (circle) each coordinating conjunction.

1. Brazil was colonized by Europeans, and its culture has been greatly influenced by this fact.

2. This was my first visit to the international section of the airport, and nothing was familiar.

3. Many people today are overweight, and being overweight has been connected to some kinds of cancer.

4. Barriers fell, markets opened, and people rejoiced in the streets because they anticipated a new life full of opportunities and freedom to make their own choices.

5. Should public school students make their own individual decisions about clothing, or should all students wear uniforms?

6. This question has been asked many times, but people are not in agreement about the ultimate punishment.

Complex Sentences

Like compound sentences, complex sentences are made up of two parts. Complex sentences, however, contain one independent clause and, at least, one dependent clause. In most complex sentences, the dependent clause is an adverb clause.

Complex Sentences (with Adverb Clauses)

Adverb clauses begin with subordinating conjunctions, which include the following:

while   although   after   because   if   before

Study the examples below. The adverb clauses are underlined, and the subordinating conjunctions are boldfaced.

The hurricane struck **while** we were at the mall.

After the president gave his speech, he answered most of the reporters' questions.

Unlike coordinating conjunctions, which join two independent clauses but are not part of either clause, subordinating conjunctions are actually part of the dependent clause.

Joe played tennis	**after** Vicky watched TV.
independent clause	dependent clause

The subordinating conjunction *after* does not connect the clauses *Joe played tennis* and *Vicky watched TV*; *after is* grammatically part of *Vicky watched TV*.

Remember that dependent clauses must be attached to an independent clause. They cannot stand alone as a sentence. If they are not attached to another sentence, they are called fragments, or incomplete sentences. Fragments are incomplete ideas, and they cause confusion for the reader. In a complex sentence, both clauses are needed to make a complete idea so the reader can understand what you mean. Look at these examples:

Fragment:	After Vicky watched TV
Complete Sentence:	Joe played tennis after Vicky watched TV.
	or
Complete Sentence:	After Vicky watched TV, she went to bed.

Study the following examples of complex sentences from the essays in this book. Draw a box around each subject, underline each verb, and circle each subordinating conjunction.

1. While the Northeast is experiencing snowstorms, cities like Miami, Florida, can have temperatures over 80 degrees Fahrenheit.

2. Although Brazil and the United States are unique countries, there are remarkable similarities in their size, ethnic diversity, and personal values.

3. Another bus arrived at the terminal, and the passengers stepped off carrying all sorts of luggage.

4. While it is true that everyone makes a blunder from time to time, some people do not have the courage to admit their errors because they fear blame.

5. Because almost every area has a community college, students who opt to go to a community college first can continue to be near their families for two more years.

Additional Grammar Activities

The three example essays in this section feature different grammatical errors. Each paragraph highlights one kind of error. In each case, read the entire essay before you complete the activities.

Before you complete Activities 1–5, read the whole essay first. Then go back and complete each activity.

ACTIVITY 1 Verb Forms

Read the paragraph and decide whether the five underlined verbs are correct. If not, draw a line through the verb and write the correct form above the verb.

Essay 2

A Simple Recipe

1   "When in Rome, do as the Romans do" may <u>sound</u> ridiculous, but this proverb <u>offer</u> an important suggestion. If you travel to other countries, especially to a country that is very different from your own, you should <u>keeping</u> this saying in mind. For example, Japan has unique customs that <u>is</u> not found in any other country. If you <u>traveled</u> to Japan, you should find out about Japanese customs, taboos, and people beforehand.

ACTIVITY 2 Verb Forms

Read this paragraph carefully. Then write the correct form of the verbs in parentheses.

2   One custom is that you should (take) _____ off your shoes before (enter) _____ someone's house. In Japan, the floor must always be kept clean because usually people (sit) _____, eat a meal, or even (sleep) _____ on the floor. Another custom

is giving gifts. The Japanese often (give) _____ a small gift
to people who have (do) _____ favors for them. Usually this
token of gratitude (give) _____ in July and December to keep
harmonious relations with the receiver. When you (give) _____
someone such a gift, you should make some form of apology about it. For
example, many Japanese will say, "This is just a small gift that I have for you."
In addition, it is not polite to open a gift immediately. The receiver usually
(wait) _____ until the giver has left so the giver will not be
embarrassed if the gift (turn) _____ out to be defective or
displeasing.

ACTIVITY 3 Connectors

Read the paragraph carefully. Then fill in the blanks with one of these connectors:

    because   in addition   even if   for example   first   but

3   _____, it is important to know about Japanese
taboos. All cultures have certain actions that are considered socially
unacceptable. _____ something is acceptable in one culture,
it can easily be taboo in another culture. _____, chopsticks
are used in many cultures, _____ there are two taboos about
chopsticks etiquette in Japan. _____, you should never stand
the chopsticks upright in your bowl of rice. _____ standing
chopsticks upright is done at a funeral ceremony, this action is associated
with death. Second, you must never pass food from one pair of chopsticks
to another. Again, this is related to burial rites in Japan.

ACTIVITY 4 Articles

There are 14 blanks in this paragraph. Read the paragraph and write the articles *a, an,* or *the* to
complete the sentences. Some blanks do not require articles.

4   Third, it is important to know that Japanese people have
_____ different cultural values. One of _____
important differences in _____ cultural values is
_____ Japanese desire to maintain _____
harmony at all costs. People try to avoid causing any kind of dispute.
If there is _____ problem, both sides are expected to
compromise in order to avoid an argument. People are expected to
restrain their emotions and put _____ goal of compromise
above their individual wishes. Related to this is _____
concept of patience. Japanese put _____ great deal of

_____ value on _____ patience. Patience also
contributes to maintaining _____ good relations with
_____ everyone **and avoiding** _____ **disputes.**

ACTIVITY 5 **Prepositions**

Read this paragraph and write the correct preposition in each blank. Choose from these prepositions:
into, in, to, about, with, of, and *around.* You may use them more than once.

5 _____ conclusion, if you want to get along well
_____ the Japanese and avoid uncomfortable situations
when you go _____ Japan, it is important to take
_____ account the features _____ Japanese
culture that have been discussed here. Although it may be hard to
understand Japanese customs because they are different, knowing
_____ them can help you adjust to life in Japan. If you face
an unfamiliar or difficult situation when you are _____
Japan, you should do what the people _____ you do. In other
words, "When _____ Japan, do as the Japanese do."

Before you complete Activities 6–12, read the whole essay. Then go back and complete each activity.

ACTIVITY 6 **Verb Forms**

Read this paragraph carefully. Then write the correct form of the verbs in parentheses.

Essay 3

Dangers of Corporal Punishment

1   What should parents do when their five-year-old child says
a bad word even though the child knows it is wrong? What should a
teacher (do) _____ when a student in the second grade
(call) _____ the teacher a name? When my parents (be)
_____ children forty or fifty years ago, the answer to these
questions was quite clear. The adult would spank the child immediately.
Corporal punishment (be) _____ quite common then. When
I was a child, I (be) _____ in a class in which the teacher got
angry at a boy who kept (talk) _____ after she told him to
be quiet. The teacher then (shout) _____ at the boy and, in

front of all of us, (slap) _____ his face. My classmates and I were shocked. Even after twenty years, I still remember that incident quite clearly. If the teacher's purpose (be) _____ to (teach) _____ us to (be) _____ quiet, she did not (succeed) _____. However, if her purpose was to create an oppressive mood in the class, she succeeded. Because corporal punishment (be) _____ an ineffective and cruel method of discipline, it should never be (use) _____ under any circumstances.

ACTIVITY 7 **Prepositions**

Read this paragraph carefully. Write the correct preposition in each blank. Use these prepositions: *in, of,* and *for.*

2 Supporters _____ corporal punishment claim that physical discipline is necessary _____ developing a child's sense _____ personal responsibility. Justice Lewis Powell, a former U.S. Supreme Court justice, has even said that paddling children who misbehave has been an acceptable method _____ promoting good behavior and responsibility _____ school children for a long time. Some people worry that stopping corporal punishment in schools could result _____ a decline _____ school achievement. However, just because a student stops misbehaving does not mean that he or she suddenly has a better sense _____ personal responsibility or correct behavior.

ACTIVITY 8 **Articles**

Read the paragraph and write the articles *a, an,* or *the* to complete the sentences. Some blanks do not require articles.

3 Corporal punishment is _____ ineffective way to punish _____ child because it may stop a behavior for a while, but it will not necessarily have _____ long-term effect. Thus, if an adult inflicts _____ mild form of _____ corporal punishment that hurts the child very little or not at all, it will not get rid of the bad behavior. Moreover, because corporal punishment works only temporarily, it will have to be repeated whenever the child misbehaves. It may then become _____ standard response to any misbehavior. This can lead to _____ frequent and more severe spanking, which may result in _____ abuse.

ACTIVITY 9 Comma Splices

Read this paragraph carefully and find the two comma splices. Correct them in one of two ways: (1) change the comma to a period and make two sentences or (2) add a connector after the comma.

4   A negative effect of corporal punishment in school is that it makes some students feel aggressive toward parents, teachers, and fellow students. In my opinion, children regard corporal punishment as a form of teacher aggression that makes them feel helpless. Therefore, students may get frustrated if corporal punishment is used frequently. Furthermore, it increases disruptive behavior that can become more aggressive, this leads to school violence and bullying of fellow students. Supporters of corporal punishment believe that it is necessary to maintain a good learning environment, it is unfortunate that the opposite result often happens. The learning environment actually becomes less effective when there is aggressive behavior.

ACTIVITY 10 Verb Forms

Read the paragraph and decide whether the underlined verbs are correct. If not, draw a line through the verb and write the correct form above it.

5   Last, corporal punishment may <u>result</u> in antisocial behavior later in life because it teaches children that adults <u>condone</u> violence as a solution to problems. Children who are <u>spank</u> learn that it is acceptable for a stronger person <u>using</u> violence against a weaker person. The concept of "might makes right" is <u>forced</u> upon them at a very early age. Furthermore, this concept teaches a lesson not only to those who are spanked but also to those who <u>witness</u> it. Studies of prisoners and delinquents <u>shows</u> that nearly 100 percent of the violent inmates at San Quentin and 64 percent of juvenile delinquents <u>was</u> victims of seriously abusive punishment during childhood. If serious punishment <u>causes</u> antisocial behavior, perhaps even milder punishment also <u>contribute</u> to violence. Research at the University of New Hampshire <u>will find</u> that children who were spanked between the ages of three and five <u>showed</u> higher levels of antisocial behavior when they <u>were observed</u> just two and four years later. This behavior included higher levels of beating family members, hitting fellow students, and defying parents. It is ironic that the behaviors for which teachers <u>punishing</u> students often get worse as a result of the spanking.

ACTIVITY 11 Editing for Errors

There are seven errors in this paragraph. They are in word forms (two), articles (one), sentence fragments (one), verb tense (one), and subject-verb agreement (two). Mark these errors and write corrections.

6   For punishment to be effective, it must produce a great behavioral change, result in behavior that is permanent, and produce minimal side effects. However, none of these changes is a result of corporal punishment. Therefore, we should consider alternatives to corporal punishment. Because discipline is necessary to educate children. One of the alternatives are to emphasize students' positive behaviors. Some research shows that reward, praise, and self-esteem is the most powerful motivators for the learning. Other alternatives are to hold conferences with students to help them plan acceptable behave or to use school staff, such as psychologists and counselors. It is important to build better interpersonal relations between teachers and students. In addition to these alternatives, instruction that reaches all students, such as detention, in-school suspension, and Saturday school, is available to discipline and punishment unruly students, too. Alternatives to corporal punishment taught children to be self-disciplined rather than to be cooperative only because of fear.

ACTIVITY 12 Editing for Errors

There are seven errors in this paragraph. They are in word forms (one), articles (three), sentence fragments (one), comma splices (one), and subject-verb agreement (one). Mark these errors and write the corrections.

7   In the conclusion, teachers should not use corporal punishment because it is ineffective in disciplining students and may have long-term negative effects on students. Moreover, teachers should not forget that love and understanding must be part of any kind of discipline. Discipline and love is not opposites, punishment must involve letting the children know that what they do is wrong and why punishment is necessary. Teachers should not just beat student with the hopeful that he will understand. It is important to maintain discipline without inflicting physical pain on students. Therefore, teachers should use effective and more humane alternatives. In order to bring about permanent behavioral changes.

Before you complete Activities 13–18, read the whole essay. Then go back and complete each activity.

ACTIVITY 13 Articles

Read the paragraph and write the articles *a, an,* or *the* to complete the sentences. Some blanks do not require articles.

Essay 4

Washington and Lincoln

1   Perhaps no other names from _____ American history are better known than the names of George Washington and Abraham Lincoln. Both of these presidents made valuable contributions to _____ United States during their presidency. In fact, one could argue that _____ America would not be _____ same country that it is today if either of these two leaders had not been involved in _____ American politics. However, it is interesting to note that although both leaders made _____ significant contributions to _____ country, they lived in _____ quite different times and served in _____ very different ways.

ACTIVITY 14 Verb Forms

Read this paragraph carefully. Then write the correct form of the verbs in parentheses.

2   Everyone (know) _____ that George Washington was the first president of the United States. What most people do not (appreciate) _____ (be) _____ that Washington (be) _____ a clever military leader. He served the country in the early days of the Revolution by (help) _____ to change the colonial volunteers from ragged farmers into effective soldiers. Without Washington's bravery and military strategy, it is doubtful that the colonies could have (beat) _____ the British. Thus, without Washington, the colonies might never even have (become) _____ the United States of America.

ACTIVITY 15 Prepositions

Read this paragraph and write the correct preposition in each blank. Choose from these prepositions: *from, in, to, with, for, between,* and *of.* You may use them more than once.

3   Abraham Lincoln was the sixteenth president _____ the United States. He was elected president _____ 1860 during a controversial and heated period of American history. As more states applied _____ membership in the growing country, the issue _____ slavery kept surfacing. There was an unstable balance _____ slave states and free states. Each time another state was added _____ the Union, the balance of power shifted. Lincoln was _____ a free state, and many _____ the slave state leaders viewed Lincoln as an enemy of their cause _____ expand slavery. _____ the end, no compromise could be reached, and the slave states seceded _____ the United States in order to form their own independent country. Hostilities grew, and _____ 1861 the Civil War, or the War _____ the States as it is sometimes called, broke out. During the next four years, the Civil War ravaged the country. By the end of the war in 1865, the American countryside was _____ shambles, but the Union was once again intact. Through his military and political decisions, Lincoln is credited _____ saving the country _____ self-destruction.

ACTIVITY 16 Editing for Errors

There are eight errors in this paragraph. They are in word forms (one), articles (two), modals (one), verb tense (two), and subject-verb agreement (two). Mark these errors and write corrections.

4   Washington and Lincoln was similarly in several ways. Both men are U.S. presidents. Both men served the United States during extremely difficult times. For Washington, the question is whether the United States would be able to maintain its independence from Britain. The United States was certainly very fragile nation at that time. For Lincoln, the question were really not so different. Would the United States to be able to survive during what was one of darkest periods of American history?

After you read this paragraph, find the three sentence fragments. Correct the fragments by (1) changing the punctuation and creating one complete sentence or (2) adding new words to make the fragment a complete sentence.

5   There were also several differences between Washington and Lincoln. Washington came from a wealthy aristocratic background. He had several years of schooling. Lincoln came from a poor background, and he had very little schooling. Another difference between the two involved their military roles. Washington was a general. He was a military leader. Became president. Lincoln never served in the military. He was a lawyer who early on became a politician. When he became president, he took on the role of commander in chief, as all U.S. presidents do. Despite his lack of military background or training. Lincoln made several strategic decisions that enabled the U.S. military leaders to win the Civil War. Finally, Washington served for two terms and therefore had eight years to accomplish his policies. Lincoln, on the other hand, was assassinated. While in office and was not able to finish some of the things that he wanted for the country.

ACTIVITY 18 Editing for Errors

There are seven errors in this paragraph. They are in articles (two), verb tense (one), inappropriate words (one), word forms (one), number (singular and plural) (one), and subject-verb agreement (one). Mark these errors and make corrections.

6   The names George Washington and Abraham Lincoln is known even to people who have never been to the United States. Both of these patriots gave large part of their lives to help America make what it is today though they served the country in very different ways in complete different time in the American history. Although they were gone, their legacies and contributions continue to have an impact on our lives.

Connectors

Using connectors will help your ideas flow. Remember that when connectors occur at the beginning of a sentence, they are often followed by a comma.

Purpose	Coordinating Conjunctions (connect independent clauses)	Subordinating Conjunctions (begin dependent clauses)	Transitions (usually precede independent clauses)
Examples			For example, To illustrate, Specifically, In particular,
Information	and		In addition, Moreover, Furthermore,
Comparison			Similarly, Likewise, In the same way,
Contrast	but	while, although	In contrast, However, On the other hand, Conversely, Instead,
Refutation			On the contrary,
Concession	yet	although though even though it may appear that	Nevertheless, Even so, Admittedly, Despite this,
Emphasis			In fact, Actually,
Clarification			In other words, In simpler words, More simply,
Reason/Cause	for	because since	
Result	so	so so that	As a result, As a consequence, Consequently, Therefore, Thus,
Time Relationships		after as soon as before when while until whenever as	Afterward, First, Second, Next, Then, Finally, Subsequently, Meanwhile, In the meantime,
Condition		if even if unless provided that when	

Purpose	Coordinating Conjunctions (connect independent clauses)	Subordinating Conjunctions (begin dependent clauses)	Transitions (usually precede independent clauses)
Purpose		so that in order that	
Choice	or		
Conclusion			In conclusion, To summarize, As we have seen, In brief, In closing, To sum up, Finally,

Useful Vocabulary for Better Writing

Try these useful words and phrases as you write your essays. They can make your writing sound more academic, natural, and fluent.

Comparing

Words and Phrases	Examples
NOUN *is* COMPARATIVE ADJECTIVE *than* NOUN.	New York *is larger than* Rhode Island.
S + V + COMPARATIVE ADVERB *than* NOUN.	The cats ran *faster than* the dogs.
S + V. *In comparison,* S + V.	Canada has provinces. *In comparison,* Brazil has states.
Although NOUN *and* NOUN *are similar in* NOUN, …	*Although* France and Spain *are similar in* size, they are different in many ways.
Upon close inspection, S + V.	*Upon close inspection,* teachers in both schools discovered their students progressed *faster* when using games.
Compared to…	*Compared to* these roses, those roses last a long time.
NOUN *and* NOUN *are surprisingly similar.*	Brazil *and* the United States *are surprisingly similar.*
The same…	Brazil has states. *The same* can be said about Mexico.
Like NOUN, NOUN *also*…	*Like* Brazil, Mexico *also* has states.
Compared to…	*Compared to* U.S. history, Chinese history is complicated.
Both NOUN *and* NOUN…	*Both* dictatorships *and* oligarchies exemplify non-democratic ideologies.
Also, S + V. / *Likewise,* S + V.	The economies in South America seem to be thriving. *Likewise,* some Asian markets are doing very well these days.
Similarly, S + V. / *Similar to* S + V.	The economies in South America seem to be thriving. *Similarly,* some Asian markets are doing very well these days.

Contrasting

Words and Phrases	Examples
S + V. *In contrast,* S + V.	Algeria is a very large country. *In contrast,* the U.A.E. is very small.
Contrasted with / *In contrast to* NOUN	*In contrast to* soda, water is a better alternative.
Although / *Even though* / *Though*…	*Although* Spain and France are similar in size, they are different in many other ways.
Unlike NOUN, NOUN…	*Unlike* Spain, France borders eight countries.
However, S + V.	Canada has provinces. *However,* Brazil has states.
On the one hand, S + V. *On the other hand,* S + V.	*On the one hand,* Maggie loved to travel. *On the other hand,* she hated to be away from her home.
S + V, *yet* S + V.	People know that eating sweets is not good for their health, *yet* they continue to eat more sugar and fat than ever before.
NOUN *and* NOUN *are surprisingly different.*	Finland *and* Iceland *are surprisingly different.*

Telling a Story/Narrating

Words and Phrases	Examples
When I was NOUN / ADJ, *I would* VERB.	*When I was* a child, *I would* go fishing every weekend.
I had never felt so ADJ *in my life.*	*I had never felt so* anxious *in my life.*
I never would have thought that…	*I never would have thought that* I could win the competition.
Then the most amazing thing happened.	I thought my bag was gone forever. *Then the most amazing thing happened.*
Whenever I think back to that time, …	*Whenever I think back to* my childhood, I am moved by my grandparents' love for me.
I will never forget NOUN	*I will never forget* my wedding day.
I can still remember NOUN / *I will always remember* NOUN	*I can still remember* the day I started my first job.
NOUN *was the best / worst day of my life.*	The day I caught that fish *was the best day of my life.*
Every time S + V, S + V.	*Every time* I used that computer, I had a problem.
This was my first NOUN	*This was my first* time traveling alone.

Showing Cause and Effect

Words and Phrases	Examples
Because S + V / *Because of* S + V	*Because of* the traffic problems, it is easy to see why the city is building a new tunnel.
NOUN *can trigger* NOUN NOUN *can cause* NOUN	An earthquake *can trigger* tidal waves and *can cause* massive destruction.
Due to NOUN	*Due to* the economic sanctions, the unemployment rate skyrocketed.
On account of NOUN / *As a result of* NOUN / *Because of* NOUN	*On account of* the economic sanctions, the unemployment rate skyrocketed.
Therefore, NOUN / *As a result,* NOUN / *For this reason,* NOUN / *Consequently,* NOUN	Markets fell. *Therefore,* millions of people lost their life savings.
NOUN *will bring about* NOUN	The use of the Internet *will bring about* a change in education.
NOUN *has had a positive / negative effect on* NOUN	Computer technology *has had both positive and negative effects* on society.
The correlation… is clear / evident.	*The correlation* between junk food and obesity *is clear.*

Stating an Opinion

Words and Phrases	Examples
Without a doubt, doing NOUN *is* ADJECTIVE *idea / method / decision / way.*	*Without a doubt,* walking to work each day *is* an excellent *way* to lose weight.
Personally, I believe / think / feel / agree / disagree / suppose that NOUN	*Personally, I believe that* using electronic devices on a plane should be allowed.
Doing NOUN *should not be allowed.*	Texting in class *should not be allowed.*
In my opinion / view / experience, NOUN	*In my opinion,* talking on a cell phone in a movie theater is extremely rude.
For this reason, NOUN / *That is why I think* NOUN	*For this reason,* voters should not pass this law.

There are many benefits / advantages to NOUN.	There are many benefits to swimming every day.
There are many drawbacks / disadvantages to NOUN.	There are many drawbacks to eating meals at a restaurant.
I am convinced that S + V.	I am convinced that nuclear energy is safe and energy efficient.
NOUN should be required / mandatory.	Art education should be required of all high school students.
I prefer NOUN to NOUN.	I prefer rugby to football.
To me, banning / prohibiting NOUN makes sense.	To me, banning cell phones while driving makes perfect sense.
For all of these important reasons, S + V.	For all of these important reasons, cell phones in schools should be banned.
Based on NOUN, S + V.	Based on the facts presented, high-fat foods should be banned from the cafeteria.

Arguing and Persuading

Words and Phrases	Examples
It is important to remember S + V	It is important to remember that school uniforms would only be worn during school hours.
According to a recent survey, S + V	According to a recent survey, 85 percent of high school students felt they had too much homework.
Even more important, S + V	Even more important, statistics show the positive effects that school uniforms have on behavior.
Despite this, S + V	Despite this, many people remain opposed to school uniforms.
S must / should / ought to	Researchers must stop unethical animal testing.
For these reasons, S + V	For these reasons, public schools should require uniforms.
Obviously, S + V	Obviously, citizens will get used to this new law.
Without a doubt, S + V	Without a doubt, students ought to learn a foreign language.
I agree that S + V; however, S + V	I agree that a college degree is important; however, getting a practical technical license can also be very useful.

Giving a Counterargument

Words and Phrases	Examples
Proponents / Opponents may say S + V	Opponents of uniforms may say that students who wear uniforms cannot express their individuality.
On the surface this might seem logical / smart / correct; however, S + V	On the surface this might seem logical; however, it is not an affordable solution.
S + V; however, this is not the case.	The students could attend classes in the evening; however, this is not the case.
One could argue that S + V, but S + V	One could argue that working for a small company is very exciting, but it can also be more stressful than a job in a large company.
It would be wrong to say that S + V	It would be wrong to say that nuclear energy is 100 percent safe.
Some people believe that S + V	Some people believe that nuclear energy is the way of the future.

Upon further investigation, S + V	*Upon further investigation,* one begins to see problems with this line of thinking.
However, I cannot agree with this idea.	Some people think logging should be banned. *However, I cannot agree with this idea.*
Some people may say (one opinion), *but I* (opposite opinion.)	*Some people may say that* working from home is lonely, *but I* believe that working from home is easy, productive, and rewarding.
While NOUN *has its merits,* NOUN…	*While* working outside the home *has its merits,* working from home has many more benefits.
Although it is true that…, S + V	*Although it is true that* taking online classes can be convenient, it is difficult for many students to stay on task.

Reacting/Responding

Words and Phrases	Examples
TITLE *by* AUTHOR *is a / an* …	*Harry Potter and the Goblet of Fire by* J.K. Rowling *is an* entertaining book to read.
My first reaction to the prompt / news / article was / is NOUN	*My first reaction to the article was* fear.
When I read / look at / think about NOUN, *I was amazed / shocked / surprised* …	*When I read* the article, *I was surprised* to learn of his athletic ability.

NOTES

NOTES

NOTES

NOTES